FASTEN YOUR SEATBELTS
THE VAN MILLER STORY

ROB R. THOMPSON

Summer Wind Press
Attica, New York

FASTEN YOUR SEATBELTS: THE VAN MILLER STORY

ISBN 9780615302065

I would like to dedicate this book to my family: To my son, Van Michael, my daughter, Cathryn, to all our grandchildren, and especially to my ever-faithful, ever-my-iron-woman, and ever-so-strong wife of fifty-seven years, Gloria.

—Van Miller

Fasten Your Seatbelts will share the life of one of the greatest voices in the history of radio. We have interviewed many who knew Van Miller the best and those interviews are transcribed for you. I wish to thank Dave Gillen and the Buffalo Broadcasters Association and Steve Cichon of staffannouncer.com.

Edited by Compass Rose

FOREWORD

It was a sparkling early September Sunday in St. Louis, and I was terrified. I was walking across the street from the Marriott Hotel in downtown St. Louis to Busch Stadium, where the Bills were getting ready to play the Cardinals. I was about three hours away from my first broadcast as the color analyst on the Bills radio network, a broadcast I had listened to since I was seven or eight years old.

I had been pressed into service after a couple of years as the pregame and halftime host on the Bills network. The longtime color man, Stan Barron, was out for the season, suffering from terminal cancer. The week before, the man the radio honchos hoped would be his replacement, a former Bills player, struggled through his first broadcast. Therefore, I was tapped as the color man to work alongside the legendary play-by-play voice of the Bills, Van Miller.

My knees were knocking as I found my way to the broadcast booth in the old Busch Stadium. My football broadcast experience consisted of high school play-by-play in Niagara County a few years before. But this wasn't Newfane vs. Wilson—this was the Big Time, the NFL.

I climbed the stairs, and when I turned the corner of the press box and entered the visitors' radio booth, I immediately relaxed. Plastered on the door of our booth, on all the walls, on the counter in front of us, and on every available flat surface, were pieces of paper with the words "ROAD ROOKIE!"

My hazing had begun. Van was welcoming me to the broadcast in the best way possible—by busting chops. It was a process that would continue for the next twenty years or so.

The Bills played miserably that day and lost to the Cardinals 37–7, netting only nine first downs. They played terribly most of that 1984 season, only winning two games, none on the road. Yet, my most vivid memories of that season were not the games, but the broadcasts, and the way Van handled them.

I was blown away by his excitement and energy level before each and every kickoff, tackle, pass, and run. It didn't matter if the Bills were on their way to the Super Bowl or on their way, as they often were, to a two win and fourteen-loss season. Van was ready, and he was jacked. Preseason, regular season, postseason—Van was always pumped up. I felt it that first day in St. Louis in 1984 and for every broadcast after that.

But the thing that made Van Miller a hall of fame broadcaster was not just the fact that he was excited. He had a gift of conveying that excitement over the air each and every Bills broadcast. When he said, "fasten your seatbelts," it wasn't phony—it was real. You knew when Van said that, something special was about to happen, something that would stick with true-blue Bills fans for a long time. And you knew that in years to come, you'd hear Van's spot-on description of the play over and over again.

Van Miller was not just the voice of the Bills; he was the *sound* of the Bills. I contend that he is what a Thurman Thomas touchdown run sounds like. He is what a Bruce Smith sack sounds like. He's what Ferguson to Butler sounds like. And I think legions of longtime Bills fans would agree with me.

Van eventually backed off the "Road Rookie" designation for me and we went on to work together for a total of sixteen seasons. Our last year together was 2003, and Van told me that summer it would be his last season.

So, fast-forward once again, to another beautiful September Sunday, this time in Orchard Park. The Bills opened the season against the New England Patriots, who, just two years prior, were Super Bowl champions. Big Sam Adams sparked a 31–0 Bills victory, with a 37–yard touchdown rumble, which had Van screaming, "Am I dreaming? Am I dreaming?" It remains one of his all-time calls, and it came in his last season of play-by-play. As far as energy and excitement, he had not lost a step, not one.

That season ended with a loss at New England, by the very same 31–0 score. Most importantly, it was Van's last broadcast. We went to dinner with the Buffalo media crew the night before in Providence, and Van entertained our party of sixteen, as well as the waitresses, cooks, and numerous on-lookers, for hours, with story after story about his years in the NFL. After the game, Van took off his headset, gave me a hug, and ended his remarkable career.

The energy level and the excitement—it was still there, right through to that final whistle of that final game in December 2003. That's what made him a hall of fame broadcaster. That's what made him the sound of the Buffalo Bills, not just the voice. That's why this book has been written. Enjoy.

John Murphy
Sports Director
WIVB-TV 4, Buffalo, New York

Van Miller is truly a man for all seasons. His career, spanning 55 years, is one of the most remarkable and versatile in the history of radio and television broadcasting. After attending Fredonia State and Syracuse University, he began his play-by-play work in basketball and football at WFCB in Dunkirk and spent the better part of five years there, with time out for a hitch in the US Army. During the Korean War, he did a three-hour, six-day-a-week morning show at WFCB. He then became Sports Director and Program Director. He broadcasted Fredonia State Basketball, did professional wrestling on radio in the era of "Gorgeous George," "Yukon Eric" and other top pro wrestlers of the time. He did quiz shows, soap box derbies, auto racing, big band music shows such as "Live with the Dorsey Orchestra," and many others. On a typical Saturday in the fall, Miller's day started at 5 a.m. and finished Sunday morning at 12:30 a.m.

In 1955 WBEN radio and TV offered him a three-month job as a summer replacement announcer. He took the job and stayed for 43 years, never missing a day's work and turning down offers from NBC, CBS and ABC to remain close to his mother in Dunkirk, who had raised him without any help. Miller did early morning TV news at Channel Four, and then took over the 6:00 p.m. and 11:00 p.m. newscasts on weekends. His play-by-play at WBEN began with the University of Buffalo basketball and football. He hosted a popular radio show, did on-camera commercial work for several sponsors, and did a high school TV quiz show, "It's Academic," for 16 years. Van also hosted a breakfast show from AM&A's and a Saturday show for teenagers at the Rendezvous Room of the Statler Hotel.

In 1960 he became the voice of the Bills, a labor of love that would extend over 37 years and make him the longest running play-by-play man with the same team in the history of the NFL. Van's calls have been used over the years on HBO, "Inside the NFL" and all three major networks, as well as ESPN and the Pro Football Hall of Fame in Canton, Ohio. On TV, he's done three different bowling shows, in addition to golf, tennis, boat racing and marathons. Miller is a member of the Western New York Sports Hall of Fame, the Chautauqua County Sports Hall of Fame, and the Buffalo Broadcast Pioneers Hall of

Fame. Miller did Bison baseball for many years, as well as Niagara University Basketball before, during and after the fabulous career of Calvin Murphy. He was the exclusive radio and TV voice of the Buffalo Braves for 8 years. Van also did NCAA and NIT tournament basketball and indoor soccer. Altogether he has broadcasted more than 2,500 games and sporting events and never missed a game.

The long-time Channel Four sports director retired from WIVB in 1998 and devoted his time to Bills play-by-play until he set aside the microphone in 2003. In 2004, NFL officials voted Van into the Pro Football Hall of Fame in Canton, Ohio by presenting him the Pete Rozelle Award, one of only twelve-network radio and TV play-by-play announcers so honored. He is a member of five Hall of Fames and in the United States Congressional Record where former Buffalo Congressman Jack Quinn paid tribute to him after his final play-by-play broadcast for the Bills. Van also played a significant role in the made-for-TV movie "Second String." Van has been married to his devoted wife Gloria for 57 years and they have two children, Cathy and Van Jr., and three grandchildren.

-New York State Broadcasters Association

CHAPTER ONE

The longer I'm away from the game; I have to believe that people are
dying off and no longer remembering me.

Don't you think people have forgotten about me?
Rob, why would people want to read about me?

Van asked those questions over and over again throughout the preparation of this book. We'd take one step forward in our work, then he'd ask them again, then we'd move ahead just a little bit more and the question would come again. I said, Van, no one has forgotten about you. That I promise. Last year as I traveled the state—someone always asked, "what's going on with Van Miller? How is he doing?"

Let me ask you: Have you forgotten about Van Miller?

Have you forgotten how he called the AFL Championship games of the mid-sixties, and how he called that Stratton on Lincoln hit heard 'round the world?

Have you forgotten how he called some of the first games after the merger?

Have you forgotten how he called the comeback game against the Houston Oilers?

Have you forgotten about wide right?

Have you forgotten his last game in 2003?

Have you forgotten about his television and radio shows "Beat the Champ," "It's Academic," or "Norman Oklahoma?"

It was a couple of years ago, 2007 to be exact when I first questioned Van about writing his story; he was—to say the very least—a bit awkward in answering and quite full of humility. There was none of the pretentious cause célèbre personality in Van Miller that many in sports and in the media carry with them. In my opinion, what you see in Van Miller is what you get. With that in mind, I was put at ease as I approached the next several months.

After that day of our first meeting, which was also the debut of Trent Edwards, we went our separate ways. I finished my work on a previous book. Christmas and the New Year came and went. And, as we watched the Arizona Cardinals snatch defeat from the jaws of victory in Super Bowl XLIII, Kendra, my wife, suggested I give Van Miller a call and see if he'd be interested in having us write his book.

"Yes, dear." I mumbled as the game ended.

It would be a couple of more months before I decided to follow my wife's advice and give Van a call. I called, and as always, he answered the phone with a wholehearted "hi ya' buddy!" For a few moments, we covered the topics of each other's holidays and general health, and then I asked again if he'd like to put his story in print. His answer was instant.

Rob, do you really think people would want to read about me? It's been a number of years. Haven't folks forgotten about me by now?

Van skirted the issue of a potential book with grace. He'd never fully say "no," and certainly never completely said "yes," but what I found most interesting was how he skirted the topic of having someone write his biography. He'd oftentimes do it with a story…one such as this, our first of many retold as close to verbatim as my Sony Digital Recorder could repeat it back to me.

Rob, let's talk about that in a couple of minutes, but have you heard this one? Have I told you this story? It's about the time Larry Felser lost his mind.

People, especially the Bills players, couldn't believe what Larry had done.

This was in the '60s, and I was called Van the Travelin' Man by many because I traveled anywhere and everywhere to broadcast just about anything. In a little bit I'll tell you about one day—my longest day—but I have to tell you about Larry Felser and one of his more troublesome headlines.

I traveled with the Bills, and on this one particular weekend the Bills were on the road. We were on our West Coast swing—we always played three games out west before returning home: Oakland, Denver, and Los Angeles, who later became the San Diego Chargers. On this one weekend, we were in Oakland to play the Raiders.

Let me say this first, though; this is important. People have to remember that the Oakland Raiders would not likely be here today—they wouldn't have had the history; they wouldn't have had the championships—if not for the generosity of Ralph Wilson.

Ralph Wilson saved the Oakland Raiders and then he saved the Boston Patriots, as well. He loaned them money, the teams were drawing badly, and, of course, in the case of the Raiders, they were in heavy competition with the Forty-Niners that were just a stone's throw away on the other side of the Bay. If Ralph Wilson hadn't done this, if he hadn't decided to save the teams from folding, the American Football League may have collapsed and the NFL altogether would look very different than it does today.

Those teams would have gone belly up, but Ralph Wilson kept the Raiders and the Patriots going until they could get a better grip. What is it? They have five Super Bowl titles between them now? When Ralph Wilson saved those teams, he essentially saved the AFL, and in my view strengthened the AFL. His getting into the Pro Football Hall of Fame is long overdue, long overdue.

Anyway, I'm skipping around some; so let me get back to the day Larry Felser lost his mind. We were on the road and had just begun a three-game road trip by playing the Oakland Raiders. This had to be sometime in the early sixties, and I was working for WBEN at the time, doing everything for BEN, as a matter of fact—I didn't have a producer, an intern, an assistant, or anyone to help me at the time. Paul Peck was my first producer but he may have not even been born yet at the time of this episode.

The game itself wasn't eventful but what happened after the game is still burned into my memory. After the game Ralph decided to throw a big dinner party for all the Bills players at one of the fancy San Francisco hotels. It was one of the biggest in town. A friend of Ralphs, Jack Tompkins was a big shot with American Airlines was also invited. So far, so good, right?

It was a great layout…all kinds of food and bottles of this that and the other was waiting for us as we get to this ballroom of this hotel.

So we all arrive—the coaches, the trainers, and most of the players, and, of course, the Buffalo media headlined by Larry Felser who worked for the Courier Express at the time. Everyone was enjoying himself or herself as food and adult beverages had begun to flow freely.

No harm, no foul.

But Jack Tompkins, unbeknownst to those of us in attendance, had also invited about thirty stewardesses from American Airlines—they were called stewardesses in those days—they were asked to come join the Buffalo Bills in some dancing and sharing of those very same adult beverages.

There were all these stewardesses amidst pro football players. Well, it didn't matter if it was all innocent or not, the headlines that Larry Felser sent back to the Buffalo Currier Express or Buffalo Evening News for the following day's reading went something like this:

"'The Bills defeat the Raiders and then danced the night away with American Airlines stewardesses.' By Larry Felser.

What! Why that headline? Now, as you can well imagine, the phone lines between Buffalo and Oakland were burning up with irate phone calls from wives, fiancées, and girlfriends. AT&T made a mint that day. Even Gloria called me, wanting to know what her Van was doing out in Oakland. I said to her, 'Gloria, I'm not doing anything, I swear to it. Just sitting on the sideline is all. Maybe I did sing a little on stage, but I'm no Fred Astaire.

I can tell you that when we finished the West Coast swing and when that flight landed back in Buffalo, it looked like Christmas had really come early. Everyone was loaded down with gifts for the women in their lives; even I was carrying a small token for Gloria, though it was an innocent evening in Oakland—platonic by every definition of the word it didn't matter. There may have certainly been the need to try to clear things up with presents. It all happened though because of that night produced by Jack Tompkins—and especially the headlines written by Larry Felser—that's why I say this was the day Larry Felser lost his mind.

Van, Ralph Wilson, and Larry Felser on the road.

I listened to the story of Larry Felser, Ralph Wilson, and those American Airlines stewardesses, not realizing until afterwards that Van still had not provided me with a definitive yes or no or even an absolute maybe as to writing his biography. Instead, I was left with only the vision of Van singing on stage, a plane full of Buffalo Bills bearing gifts, and the tarmac at the Buffalo International Airport filled with irate wives and significant others.

What has proven to be interesting is how Van skirted that and other topics. He often did it with one of these stories from his NFL career and then, when he was done, he'd say get back to him about the question still lying on the table. This process repeated itself for several months, and after some growing frustration I tried to find a different way to ask the same question. It was early spring of 2009 and I tried again, and this time Van asked *me* a question.

Do you think people will want to read about me? Do you think that I have anything to say that will interest people? It seems that the longer I'm away from the game, the more people are dying off and forgetting about me.

Again, it is my opinion, but one that is well founded. I don't think anyone has or will ever forget about Van Miller. If you have been a fan of the Bills since their founding in the sixties, or if you had seen the merger and the gray days of the seventies, and if you had suffered through the painful eighties *and* the Super Bowl years of the nineties, you could never forget about the voice that made for you those memories.

If, however, you are a new fan of the Buffalo Bills, you need to be introduced to the voice that, as John Murphy said so well in the foreword, sounded like a Thurman Thomas run, a Jim Kelly pass, or a Mike Stratton hit. To the new or young fan of the Buffalo Bills, it's time for you to meet your Uncle Van.

---

*Larry Felser is a longtime sports writer, first with the *Buffalo Courier Express* and later with the *Buffalo Evening News*. He covered every one of the first thirty-seven Super Bowls prior to his retirement. He has been a strong advocate for former players of the American Football Conference admission into the Pro Football Hall of Fame, and has authored the book *The Birth of the NFL: How the 1966 NFL/AFL Merger Transformed Pro Football*.

CHAPTER TWO

*I—we, Gloria and I—have so many wonderful memories and so many special moments.
We have been very, very blessed in life.*

"Special moments…"

Those two words were important in getting to know Van Miller, though I failed to immediately recognize that fact. Our banter went on for several more months. Each time I'd call Van and I would chat about this, that, and other things, and I would eventually get around to asking him about writing a book. He was clearly apprehensive.

Van would dodge the question as if it was a high and in fastball, yet in his own way he would answer his own question about being remembered by relaying some moment or some accomplishment from his life in radio and television. He was cautious because he had had a previous negative experience with a biographer. I didn't want to be a second negative for him and Gloria.

The more I called, the more he talked and the more I listened. Perhaps the more I peppered him with the question, the more Van eventually realized that a book was a possibility and, as I had mentioned, a necessity. Or, what I think is more likely, is that Van knew all along that he wanted to be part of a book and he simply enjoyed entertaining me with the stories. These stories—these people, these places and events that he told me about—created the framework of the Van Miller story—*not* the heart of who he is, but the framework. NBA Hall of Famer Bob McAdoo shared this with me and he was so right.

Rob there is so many stories about Van, and so much that should be said. Van simply enjoys sharing all that he has done with everyone and he draws folks in with his incredible sense of humor.

But if Van wouldn't come out and openly commit to a project, what was I going to do? Getting him to commit to his biography was going to be a mighty challenge. I also discovered and as many have told me, Van Miller is a very private person. There is the public persona, the voice behind the microphone and in front of the television camera, and then there is the private Van Miller. I had to be very careful even in the most casual of conversations not cross too much into his private life.

I have conducted many interviews, there have been ones with very public people—celebrities, some would call them—and during these I had to hold a high degree of professionalism in my approach. Above all, I could not appear nervous or star struck, which, unfortunately, I have fallen victim to on several prior occasions. Those interviews were structured and well rehearsed and the results were pretty well known before I ever sat down with the subject, the interview was just a formality.

Van Miller is most certainly a celebrity; he is in many halls of fame and no one has done more in radio and television than he has. So how would I approach him? How would I talk to him? Would I have well-manicured statements filled with catalogs of footnotes and blathering pages of minutia? Is that something that would make him feel comfortable and more willing to talk?

Through much trial and error, I have learned the best way to get the flow of information started was to ask leading questions. In other words, ask questions that began with "how," "why," and "what." I learned never to ask a yes or no question, and yet that's just what I had been doing with Van when questioning him regarding writing his book: yes or no? I expected Van to answer "yes" he will or "no" he wouldn't agree to a biography, and that wasn't realistic—a big mistake on my part. I expected him to provide one-word answers and worse to be just as structured as I was. That was even a bigger mistake. I don't think any of us can give a simple yes or no answer to most questions that we're ever asked, and Van couldn't either. I was expecting him to say yes, for us to sit down on five preordained occasions, for him to answer a scripted list of boring questions, and for the book to be completed and to sell 10,000 copies—just like that. I assumed this would be a very structured project. Well, we all know what is said about those that assume.

As my frustration was growing it was a tremendous relief to learn that Van is not scripted in any way, shape or form so I couldn't be scripted in my job or we would have great difficulty with our project. I had to relax, to enjoy the setting and the conversation and, most importantly, enjoy our host and hostess.

Let me share with you the first time I met Van Miller, it was at a Buffalo Bills game. The Bills, had granted us press box passes, and it was the same game where Trent Edwards was making his debut as the Bills starting quarterback. And, as fate had it, our seats were next to Van's. We struck up a conversation right away. Van, my wife, and I discussed everything from bad football to bad jokes but we also talked about Bills' history, and, as the third quarter drew to a close he had told us many short, wonderful stories. I took a shot in the dark and I posed the awkward yes or no question regarding such an idea as writing his story. We stared at each other across a plate of leftover press box nachos; he didn't provide an answer, just his phone number, and said that I could call him anytime. We returned to watching the game.

There was a TV timeout. Then Van continued to share, in his own unique way, the entirety of all that he had done during the course of his career, one morsel at a time—bits and pieces of stories about people, places, and games. It wasn't necessarily in any particular order, but he began to tell me his story in dribs and drabs.

Rob, no one has done more in the history of radio and television than I have.

To be honest I wasn't sure what that meant and since I didn't have a recorder with me that day I scribbled notes as best I could, and the end result resembled the works of a Jackson Pollock-Pablo Picasso hybrid. The game that day had drifted to the latter part of the second half; Trent Edwards was having a pretty good debut, and Van stood frequently to slowly do some stretching exercises during team or TV timeouts.

I had a couple bad accidents as a teenager, one time breaking my back so I always stretch. The accidents ended my playing sports but may have started my interest in broadcasting sports. I've been blessed as a result. Rob, no one has done more in radio than me and as a result I—we, Gloria and I—have had many, many special moments together.

I was compiling mental notes of key Van Miller words and phrases; however, it would be those *two* words that I would choose to focus on throughout the course of the writing: "special moments." They were, simultaneously, specific *and* generic in meaning, for when he wanted to expand on a topic we were discussing, he would do so without feeling pressured into doing so.

"Special moments…"

I repeated those words several times on that day, and have done so frequently in preparing this book.

"Special moments…"

What were those special moments that he was speaking of?
I let my imagination go for a ride right there in the press box.
As my wife Kendra watched Steve Tasker, and as the press box watched the Bills defeat the New York Jets (Edwards going 22–28 for 234 yards), I watched Van and tried to see *all* that he had seen.

"Special moments…"

Could they be a game…the Super Bowls? What about the comeback game that *had* to be a special moment.
The game against the Jets ended and we said our good-byes, and I thought nothing else of it other than it, too, was just another one of those special moments for Kendra and me. I finished my previous non-fiction work and satisfied deadlines for a subsequent novel but Van Miller was never far from me. Those words he used, special moments have echoed since he first mentioned them to me and as I initially interpreted them as the most obvious of ones—the AFL Championship games, the comeback game, the four consecu-

tive Super Bowls, and his own induction into the Pro Football Hall of Fame. What could be more special than those?

Some of the modern-era personalities, their public accomplishments are what make them who they are. It's not so with Van Miller. I saw, rather quickly, that by setting aside my football moment assumptions it became just that much clearer what Van's special moments might have been. If you, the readers, were in his shoes what do you think those could be?

I do think that those words—*special moments*—are a significant prelude to not only Van Miller's story, but to all of our own very unique stories.

I wanted to know, as best I could, anyway, just what Van's core was all about. If I discovered what it was my task might prove easier. So for a few pages allow me to deviate in order to make a point.

Van Miller is approximately the age my father would have been if he had made it past November of 1978. I look at Van as I do my father. Van is certainly one of the most well known faces in not only the greater Buffalo area but in the history of broadcasting while my father wasn't. I have come to wonder about what their lives, Van and my father's boyhood years would have been like.

What were Van's special moments as a boy?

What made him happy?

What made him enjoy life?

What made him laugh?

In such reflection, I couldn't help but be taken back to the years of their youth and hope that by better understanding those years I'd better understand not only my father but also Van Miller. The decade of the twenties was or had to be formative for both of them. It was a decade of tremendous technological birth and expansion. It was a decade of historical firsts, and it was a time where great wealth had economic ruin nipping at its heels.

I envision the decades of the twenties and thirties as John Steinbeck painted it in any number of his novels, mainly, though, I see that period of time through the eyes of *The Grapes of Wrath*. I saw a nation at its finest and worst all at once. As I hunt and peck across this keyboard, I have wondered if the experiences of the Joad family, and Van Miller were at all similar.

What stands out about the characters of the Joad family as portrayed by Henry Fonda and Jane Darwell, is their calmness, their dedication to family, and their resoluteness through every conceivable difficulty. Traits that Van said made *his* mother and grandmother iron women. Jack Kemp said to me, not many months before his death:

Rob everyone worked hard...everyone was committed to succeeding and taking care of their families and their neighbors. The Buffalo Bills of the '60s were committed to success and everyone knew Van was totally dedicated to being the best at what he did and that sense of commitment may in fact have come from growing up in the Depression Era.

The generation from which Van comes is unique and those words, *special moments,* used with purposeful casualness by Van Miller, had made me a bit melancholy when I thought of my father, mother, or my so recently-passed sister. Van has seen a lot in his life. He has taken everything apparently in stride and as so many have said he has never been fazed by difficult moments.

I also saw just what an impact those words *special moments* had on Van as he spoke of his own mother and grandmother. Without knowing it, those two simple words had given this book the much-needed kick-start to his biography. Having watched Van during our interviews—*his* eyes, *his* body language—I do believe that, for him, some of his fondest moments are not football-related, but they are the memories he carries with him of his mother and grandmother.

Rob, they were iron women without question.

The way his voice shook and the way his eyes watered when he spoke of them made it quite clear that they and, along with his wife, Gloria, and children, Cathryn and Van Michael are the most special. To this casual onlooker, they are what helped mold the clay that gave to us all Van Miller. Their calmness and resoluteness through great difficulty gave us Van and Van gave us many of our own *special* moments.

Isn't it true, that our lives are filled with one special moment after another? I know for me, the older I grow the more I'm reminded of just how profound simple statements like this one can be. Simple statements like "stop and smell the roses" and "for God's sake, let bygones be bygones" have a greater meaning when realize that more years now rest behind me than in front of me. Many times over the years, I have been told that our lives are just one giant jigsaw puzzle; it's not until we near our final days on Earth, when all the pieces have been fit into place that we become aware of what the picture is.

With our birth, all the pieces of life's puzzle are dumped out on the floor in front of us and we are clueless as to what to do with them. Each piece of this puzzle is literally just one *special moment* after another. At first we learn to creep and stumble along, trying to fit the pieces into place regardless of whether or not they fit. We often grow frustrated when these pieces go astray or are lost or damaged, and many times we want to give up; yet it is our job, with painstaking patience, to fit these pieces together and to gradually reveal our life's picture.

The years go by and some pieces begin to fit and our appreciation for things other than ourselves begins to grow. As we age, we may recall one or more of these *pieces* more than others—or one *piece* may have more of a dominant role than some others—these become our *special moments.*

Without delving too far into the world of the esoteric and separating greatly from the topic at hand, doesn't it seem that the younger we are, the newer life's puzzle is? We are more apt to say we'll "finish it tomorrow" or "I don't care what the 'puzzle' looks like." Jack Kemp once told me that when we are young every day is a brand-new adventure. Another former Bills quarterback Joe Ferguson; who has battled cancer now for several years said this:

Rob I wish the young would slow down and enjoy life. Life was much different for me as a kid and certainly had to be for Van.

When *I* was young, the world was great and wondrous and full of fanciful, flowery gardens; the trees were full, and bubbling over with lemon drops. My image may be over the top, but I do believe that's how the young view the world. Joe Ferguson is correct. Are they, the young as prepared for the difficult moments of life as was Van? Are they as prepared as his mother was?

Life became a reality for me as soon as I moved away from my parents' home. On my own I struggled. There are many trial and error moments. Why was I so confused and why did I make so many mistakes?

Is it because I had *too* many choices in life? Is it because I didn't know which choice to make or which way to go? Our fathers and mothers had far fewer choices than we did. In the case of my father, and perhaps Van, and certainly many others of their generation, they had few *pieces* to choose from early on in their lives so, though they had fewer choices, their picture *was* much clearer—even at an early age. What their life was going to be or the general direction it would go was pretty much determined long before their schooling ended.

My father wanted to be a pharmacist, but that wasn't to be for him. He was an only child left to the care of his mother, both abandoned at the outbreak of The Great Depression; this is why Van Miller reminds me of my father in so many ways. Work was my father's only choice, and even what type of work he could do was very limited. He made the best of what he had, and as he told us towards the end of his life, his special moments were centered on being able to see his children whenever he could. He was calm and resolute to the very end.

The generations that have followed my father's have certainly changed. Now, *special* moments for many are centered on things. Just recently I heard a young man, perhaps high school age say that the greatest moment of his life was getting a new four-wheeler.

Are special moments now just too commonplace and therefore taken for granted? Is it because we believe that another special moment is right around the corner? Or is it because they happen so very often that they are no longer seen as unique or meant for us? Or perhaps worse, is it that in today's world we are so busy trying just to survive that we don't recognize the significance of each and every day in our lives?

What exactly is it that makes a day, a week, or a year unique? Especially now, in this day and age, where everything has become *so* commonplace and the purchase of a four-wheeler is a life-changing event. Are special moments still a new relationship, birth of a child, or a key moment in time that makes all of us swallow just a bit more in pride.

Is the flag being raised on Iwo Jima still special?

Is the flag being raised on the surface of the moon still special?

Or is it the flag being draped over the shoulders of Jim Craig, after the Americans defeated the Russians at that Lake Placid Olympics? Or is Whitney

Houston's rendition of the National Anthem—still the best—a special moment?

On a larger, more historical scale, how many of these *special moments* have we seen in our lives? What about your parents? How about your grandparents? How many did they see?

Now I have to ask for your tolerance again, for just few moments, a couple of additional pages at most, to demonstrate how much the world and, therefore, life can change in one person's lifetime with the accumulation of these *special moments.*

Rob, Gloria—my wife and I—have had so many special moments.

What have they, Van and Gloria seen in their life together? How much has the world changed since they were young, compared to now? Regardless of whether we really believe it or not, all of us and all that we do each and every moment of each and every day matters a great deal in the overall scheme of things. We too, therefore, are pieces, the *ultimate* pieces, in life's puzzle. In other words, what my great grandfather did eighty years ago affected his day or a day of someone else and that in turn affected others. The legendary Bills linebacker Darryl Talley said this:

I grew up in a large city, we played in the streets and did normal kid stuff, and the world changed a lot for me. If you were to compare the '50s to the '90s it was two different worlds. Van Miller was from the older generation but regardless of how the world changed or how much the game changed he was always comfortable with it.

Let me start this example by using the year 1927. My father, a disabled little boy, was six years, and my mother, the youngest of three girls, had turned three in August of that year. My father was raised in Rochester, New York, my mother in Swanton, Vermont. One thing after another, one event after another, had to occur each year, month, weekday, and hour for that little boy and that little girl to meet as adults and to begin their family. If they had not met and moved to where they had, I would have never met *my* wife, and someone else may be tapping this story across the screen of their own Dell.

Did my parents know what course their life would take after they met?

Did they know they'd marry and have five children?

Did they know that he would die in his son's arms, and some twenty-five years later, she would be called home a continent away? No, of course not, they had to set out to put their own puzzle together as a couple and accept what life gave them.

Let's again return to the year 1927. Let us also say, that my great grandfather turned eighty years old that year; what would *he* have experienced in his lifetime? What people, places, things or events might he have taken for granted as his days clicked on by? What would have taken place over the course of those eighty years that would have changed his life for the better or for the worse, and therefore changed what he did?

Grandpa Thompson would have seen in his eighty years nineteen American presidents, ranging from James K. Polk through to the administration of Calvin Coolidge, and he would have seen the assassination of three of them—Lincoln, Garfield, and McKinley. Merton Sydney would have lived through four wars, from the Mexican-American War, the Civil War, and the Spanish-American War right up to World War One. He would have also seen a very unofficial war take place across the western plains against the American Indians. He would have heard about Joshua Chamberlain's defense of Little Round Top, George Custer's fall at Little Big Horn, and Teddy Roosevelt's charge up San Juan Hill. He, too, would have heard about 5,000 Allied losses at the Battle of Scimitar Hill during the First World War. During his years, he would have witnessed the doings of Generals Grant, Lee, Jackson, and Meade, and "Black Jack" Pershing.

He would have seen his own ancestors…his predecessors travel the roads in everything from the stagecoach to the Model T, and he would have heard about man's increased ability at self-destruction with the use of the Gatling gun, the "potato masher" (a type of hand grenade), and the tank. He would have seen the birth and the progression of air travel. From the early days of manned balloon flight and manned gliders to headlines about the exploits of Edward Rickenbacker and Manfred von Richthofen, "The Red Baron." He would have borne witness to the change in his world from pasteurization of milk to chemical warfare and from the internal combustion engine to the sinking of the unsinkable Titanic. During the course of his life, Merton would have seen the invention of the drinking straw, the matchbook, the sewing machine, and toilet paper.

In 1847, when my Great Grandfather Thompson was born, there were 29 states, and when he turned eighty in 1927, there were 48 States. In 1847, there was The Kingston Buggy Company from North Carolina churning out buckboards, and in 1927, Detroit Michigan celebrated the last of the Model T's. In 1847, it would often take families three, four, or even five months to cross the continental United States. Just eighty years later, in 1927, Charles Lindbergh flew solo from New York to Paris in just over thirty-three hours, traveling per hour what eighty years before would take a week. In 1847, baseball was a twinkle in a bored person's eye, and in 1927, Ty Cobb had hit number 4,000. In 1847, the doughnut was created; postage stamps were a nickel, and Stephens Foster's "Oh, Susanna" was performed for the very first time. In 1927, Henry Ford paid his workers a dollar a day, bread was nine cents a loaf, and the pop-up toaster was invented. In 1847, Fredrick Douglas published the first issue of *The North Star*. In 1927, the Harlem Globetrotters played their very first game. Born in 1847, along with ol' Grandpa Thompson, were Alexander Graham Bell, Thomas Edison, and Jesse James. Born in 1927 were Gina Lollobrigida, the Holy Father, Pope Benedict XVI, and former head coach of the Buffalo Bills, Johnny Rauch.

All these were momentous occasions and in one way, shape, or form they all changed life just a little bit, or perhaps they changed it a great deal...but regardless it was changed.

This, of course, is just a sampling of what was experienced in *one* lifetime...that of my grandfather's. I didn't include literature, other forms of science, or medicine, architecture, agricultural, or even anthropological advances.

Now if a person from Buffalo, Attica, or even Dunkirk was born in 1927, what would they have experienced in their lifetimes by the time they blew out their eighty birthday candles in 2007?

They would have seen the oath of office taken by fourteen additional American presidents, and they would have seen the assassination of yet another.

They would have seen the Second World War to end all wars, as well all those that followed it, The Korean War, The Viet-Nam War, The First Gulf

War, and The Second Gulf War. They would have witnessed the activities of Generals Patton, MacArthur, Westmoreland, and Schwarzkopf.

As a child, he or she would have enjoyed the benefits from the advances made by their grandparents, one of them being radio. On radio, they would have spent their evenings listening to *Major Bowes and His Original Amateur Hour*, *The Jack Benny Show*, and *Amos and Andy*. Just a number of years later, as an adult, they would have watched a new fad called television deliver *Amos and Andy*, *The Jack Benny Show*, and *I Love Lucy* to their living rooms.

As a young child or teenager, they would have ridden in or even learned to drive in a 1927 Packard Roadster or a Studebaker Sedan. As an adult, they would have traveled in a DeSoto, AMC Rambler, Chevy Nova, and perhaps even a 2001 Windstar minivan.

My grandparents and, to some degree, my parents, would have seen the refinement of radio, television, talking motion pictures, automobiles, airplanes and space travel. They would have also seen the invention of the Iron Lung, PEZ Candy, Bubble Gum, and the parking meter, and for better or worse, the creation of the A-bomb, the H-bomb, and the Tomahawk Missile. They, too, would have seen the cure for polio.

They would have read the headlines declaring everything from Pearl Harbor to 9-11 and from John Glenn to Apollo 11, the space shuttle, and the landing on Mars by unmanned spacecraft. As my mother told me seemingly every time, with her VCR forever blinking twelve in the background, the world is advancing far greater than she could ever have thought it possible, both above and below her feet. You readers now in your forties, *my* age, think about how much things have changed from the time we were riding our banana seat bikes and watching cartoons.

All these events, the people, the places and things that have taken place in our parents', grandparents', our own; and in our children's lives are pieces of that overall puzzle we have mentioned. They are what have helped make us and they are the seeds that help us add to the ever-changing world.

They are special moments, yet did the historical moments make our grandparents' special moments or did our grandparents make history special? It's the chicken or the egg but what is obvious is that the older generation, our grandparents have made our lives far easier and much more enjoyable. They have provided for us many more options from which to choose to live work and be entertained. The more advanced our nation became, the greater our thirst was to be entertained.

When America became less of an agrarian nation and suburbia was born, so too was the 9–5 Monday through Friday lifestyle of the American family. Technology shortened the workdays for the average American; no longer were there 12–14 hour shifts, at least mandatory ones. With greater wages and more work choices, the opportunity for advanced education increased.

Workers learned more skills and wages increased, not always commensurate with these skills, but they increased none-the-less. Shorter workweeks + longer lives + increased disposable income = a desire to be entertained. They, our parents and grandparents, wanted to be entertained, and entertained more than at any other time in our nation's history. Not only did these advances in technology make the work lives of Americans easier, new technology gave them advances in motion pictures, radio, and television. Technology therefore made Americans more social.

With life being made easier, or as some would say, better, Americans had more free time on their hands. And because we tend to be a fickle people, advances had to be made in the areas of entertainment to keep pace with the demand of the social needs of the bored American. Sitting around the radio twice a week to catch the scrambled signal of an hour-long variety show wasn't going to be enough. People were learning more, making more, and spending more, so they expected more. Just how would this and subsequent generations of Americans be entertained?

There was a clear demand for entertainment, but how and what would entertain a growing populace of the bored and fickle? Would literature, hobbies, or the ability for easy travel become the entertainment fix? This need/desire to be entertained brought about the advances in new forms of art—talking motion pictures and radio had been advancing for many years. In addition, just prior to World War Two, television was born; and that small screen would shrink America that much more. Dare I say here that if agrarian America had not shrunk in the way that it had, and this nation's cities had not boomed, mass entertainment might not have flourished when it did.

Perhaps if we were still a nation predominantly made up of farmers, Charlie Chaplin would never have walked like a penguin in silent pictures. Perhaps if the train were never delivered to us, then east would have never met west...if this and if that and if the other. So, as confusing as this chapter of examples may have been for you, and I do apologize it if was, I hope that we have shown that all these series of special moments and events that took place from the days of our great grandparents on did allow Chaplin to walk us from the silent picture to the talkies.

The train led to the plane and the covered wagon led to the station wagon and jugglers led to vaudeville and vaudeville to silent pictures and the telegraph led...well...perhaps it led to radio.

Chaplin handed the baton to Al Jolson, and the first talking movie, *The Jazz Singer* was introduced to us in exchange for a handful of pennies. After World War Two, talking pictures evolved from the big movie house screens into smaller living room television screens, exploding all over the country. For some who had their careers thrive on radio, the transition to television was relatively painless. There was Jack Benny, Lucy, and Jackie Gleason, and sports broadcasting boomed to life with some of the greatest names of all time sparking the imagination of youth around the nation...particularly one young man from Dunkirk New York. Television united the west coast and east coast far quicker than the golden spike had and Ed Sullivan introduced us to the lads from Liverpool and the quite boy from Memphis.

Early radio and television had quenched the initial thirst to be entertained. But if not for radio, where would television be? Radio and television were escapisms when other avenues of escape were still out of reach. Television and radio brought America's sports scene to homes all across the nation; there were now fans of the New York Yankees and Boston Red Sox all over the states. They seemed a perfect match—sports and radio—for one another, and for us here in Western New York, Van Miller is the voice of *that* sports scene; he is, as John Murphy said, what a Thurman Thomas run sounds like.

If not for radio...

If not for Van Miller...

If not for so many things, so many other things would not have happened. If events, people, and things had not happened in a specific way at a specific time, we would not have had radio, Van may not have claimed Western New York as home, and radio and Van Miller may never have met. We are thankful that they did meet though. We should now ask what has Van seen in his lifetime, and how has he made all our lives better just for knowing him?

In time I began to see what Van had seen. I never again asked if he wanted a book written. There were no more yes or no questions; there was no more formality to our time together. What follows over the next few chapters is a conversation between two friends and with someone who so greatly reminds me of my own father, so please enjoy our chat.

CHAPTER THREE

I don't know what I would have done
if radio hadn't come along...after all I couldn't dance.

We have talked about everything except your questions, we should move forward. Rob, in all my broadcasting years, there are two words I never used 'forward progress;' it's crazy—what exactly does forward progress mean? It is redundant. Is there such a thing as backward progress? I ask you again, it is redundant, is it not? Too many times you will hear announcers and officials butcher the King's English when they use words or phrases such as 'forward progress.'

Naturally, everyone make mistakes; Joe Theisman, a nice guy to be sure, and someone who has become a pretty good broadcaster after he retired from the league, he is a real nice personable person—from Notre Dame, so nothing less is expected, right? The former Redskin quarterback once said during a game, 'There are no geniuses in football; there are no Marvin Einstein's what-so-ever in the NFL. He was trying to make a point while being self-deprecating at the same time. I, even I, Uncle Van, once made a mistake when I was reporting the baseball scores one night. I told the viewers that tonight the Kansas Shitty Royals had defeated the New York Yankees.

Van, that's not bad, because for a long time they were the Kansas Shitty Royals.

I can't say that now, but maybe they weren't the best the American League had to offer at the time. In baseball, the American League has to be considered, as the home of some of the greatest teams and players ever to play. All one has to do is look at the New York Yankees and Boston Red Sox to see that.

Van was right of course. In returning to our little scenario, what else had Van seen by the time he had celebrated his eightieth birthday in 2007? How much has the world changed for him in those eighty years?

He would have seen the admission of Hawaii and Alaska as our forty-ninth and fiftieth states; no longer was the United States an "isolated" nation, his country was a preeminent player on the world stage.

He has benefited from man's advancement in areas of medicine, science, civil rights, and the arts. Yet he also has witnessed the worse side of man expand in many of the same areas. Van has seen man attempt to eliminate his fellow man in faraway places, such the gulags, Auschwitz, and the Killing Fields of Cambodia.

Van and his peers, would have seen the heartland of this nation torn asunder by the dust bowl and would have seen America and most parts of the world devastated by the Depression of the thirties.

Since World War One wasn't the war to end all wars, they would have likely served in the next immediate war to end all wars that engulfed most of the world in the forties. The shrinking world would have shown them that one man; Hitler——had killed millions in the name of purity. Also, they would have seen for the first time hundreds of thousands die from just one bomb.

They would have lost family and friends in Korea, Viet Nam, Gulf War I, and Gulf War II. And they would fail in finding the right words to describe how they felt after Pearl Harbor and 9-11.

As the years passed they would have seen the courage of Martin Luther King, Jr. as he marched on Selma and they would have seen the early career of the nation's first African-American Chief Executive.

They would have borne witness to a presidential resignation, a presidential impeachment, the hippies, the Lindbergh kidnapping, the kidnapping of Patty Hearst, the Manson murders, Son of Sam, the Zodiac Killer, the Boston Strangler, and the Hillside Strangler.

They would have witnessed the assassination attempt of Presidents Gerald Ford and Ronald Reagan and of Pope John Paul II. They would have seen the birth of rock 'n' roll, the arrival of The Beatles, and they would have seen the murder of John Lennon and the untimely death of Elvis Presley.

Van *has* seen the flag raised on Iwo Jima and on the surface of the moon. He would have listened to Franklin Roosevelt's fireside chats, *Buffalo Bob, The Shadow Knows,* and to Neil Armstrong's words, "one small step for man, and one giant leap for mankind." A person born in 1927 would have seen America's game, baseball, in its heyday with Ruth, Gehrig, Mantel, and Williams, and they would have seen its desegregation as Jackie Robinson took to second base.

Van would have likely have gone for a ride in a Packard Roadster, then a Studebaker Sedan. His first car was a 1941 Pontiac while others may have owned a Dodge convertible, followed by an AMC Rambler, Chevy Nova, Acura Legend, and even a Ford Windstar with one hubcap missing. They would have walked to school carrying a McGuffey reader. Their children would have driven to school and their grandchildren would be going to class online.

Van has lived through some extraordinary times. From days traveling Route 66 following John Steinbeck's dust to cross-country and cross-oceanic flights. He has seen missions to the international space station and even to the furthest points of our galaxy, and the ever-so-real, ever-so-illogical tension of mutual obliteration of the Cold War. Van has seen everything from early radio and early talking motion pictures to…well to what we *all* see today.

As a kid I always had fun despite it all. I didn't know we were poor we just lived day to day. My mother and grandmother worked hard everyday and their enjoyment, what made them laugh was watching me do an imaginary broadcast from our front yard. I probably listened to sports before I ever played baseball or basketball. Radio is really what introduced me to the excitement of a game. The announcers delivered that excitement to me. If not for radio and sports I don't know what I would have done.

The times had changed and as we have discussed there was so much more for us to do and much more free time in which to do it. Just how though would Americans spend all this new free time and how would they spend their ever-increasing amount of disposable income?

Would they spend a couple of bucks on a movie, perhaps a ball game? Baseball was *still* America's game, but since the conclusion of the nineteenth century, another game had been emerging as a fan favorite. Football was born, sometime around 1870 to 1880—the date isn't too relevant, though some other authors would differ on that. But for what we are discussing now, let us say 1875 was its birthday. Football was seen as an American bastardization of Rugby; but soon, quite soon, it was drawing crowds far larger than baseball's. Football, again according to some of the game's historians, was born on the campus yards of Yale or Harvard, and let us not leaves out Columbia or Brown. The game, as it became more popular, was nurtured to a more uniform game with new ideals and rule changes.

Professional baseball was still king while professional football was in its infancy in 1927, but it was full of life on university campuses across the nation. College teams were playing before tens of thousands of fans from Illinois to Minnesota, from Georgia to the military academies. Harvard and Yale had begun their rivalry years before. Ohio and Michigan. Minnesota and Purdue. And one of the biggest games was always the Notre Dame *Ramblers* versus just about anyone else. Notre Dame was the original "America's Team." But why Notre Dame?

Rob, Notre Dame was—and I have to agree with you—the first real America's Team, long before the Dallas Cowboys claimed that title. They had great players, of course…the era of Knute Rockne and the Four Horsemen emboldened the imaginations of many kids around the country and the way the games were called emboldened me to call those imaginary games into our front yard garden hose.

Do you think Notre Dame was so popular because it was a Catholic school and the nation was, so I've been told, predominantly Catholic at the time?

I think the large Catholic population helped to make the school's football program popular, for sure. Knute Rockne was memorable…the movie with Ronald Reagan as George Gipp—who could ever forget that 'win one for the Gipper' scene? But Notre Dame football has, I think, always has been popular regardless of the era. Ara Parseghian of the seventies and Lou Holtz—he was one of the best coaches they had. Lou Holtz is one of the most successful coaches in college football history too. He led Notre Dame to a national title in the late eighties. Rob, besides I was a good little Catholic boy growing up in Dunkirk, so I had to listen and cheer for Notre Dame, and so when I pretended to call a game using an egg beater Notre Dame never lost a game---at least in my imagination.

I have to wonder—myself a converted Catholic—if Notre Dame's popularity was due to its religious heritage or was the popularity of its football program due to the Catholic versus Protestant attitude that may have permeated across the stands of these Notre Dame versus everyone else games.

Notre Dame football was unrivaled at the time of its success—perceived or actual—and in its fan base. But don't tell that to any Michigan alum.

My understanding of both Catholic and football history during the decade of the twenties, tells me that it was because Notre Dame was a Catholic school that made its football popular. When a program became popular, its personalities became popular and almost mythical. Mythical players and coaches broadened the teams' fan base, as well as those the base of those who disliked the school. Rivalries, *national* rivalries, grew with intensity. It was an era that saw the soon-to-be renamed "Fighting Irish" accomplish an overall .800 winning percentage and an overall record of 105–12 between the years 1918 and 1930. Everybody loves a winner and Notre Dame was a winner.

The Rockne era was colorful; as Van said, we have all seen the Ronald Reagan/George Gipp performance. Football was alive and it was full of fanciful, magnificent characters that would become some of the first real-life gridiron heroes. These heroes weren't in a far-off distant land; they were as close as our imagination and as close as the radio brought them. The era was one in which the players were being emulated by youngsters from coast to coast, in sandlot games, and it was an era where even the games were being rebroadcast from the imagination of a young Van Miller.

Though baseball may have still been king, football had begun to satisfy the sports-hungry entertainment audiences across the nation, and Knute Rockne seemed a likely first national hero of the game for many—in particular, Van. If not for Notre Dame football, would we have ever listened to Van Miller on a Sunday afternoon? If not for that Dunkirk garden hose would he have told us about the comeback?

Rob, when I was a little kid, I was six or seven years old—probably older—I would stand out in our front yard holding a spoon or shouting into the end of a garden hose calling

Notre Dame games. They never lost, not once—I'd see to it. It was listening to those games that became my escape, I guess; it was my entertainment. I made mom and my grandmother laugh, so I guess I entertained them, too when there might have been very little to laugh about.

It was listening to those games and to those announcers of the day that I picked up on some of the early skills on how to call a game. I practiced play-by-play. I wore my mother and grandmother out, I think, but they always laughed, too, at what I did and how I did it. I was seven years old, or six maybe, but I called those games every weekend. And when they weren't playing, I'd do the rebroadcast of them…with a better outcome, of course, if they had, God forbid actually lost. I did it on our porch, in our living room, from the neighbors' front yard—everywhere—I'm sure the neighbors were growing worried, but they did enjoy themselves, too. So they always said.

There were so many days where I would listen to the game and if I wasn't happy with the call or, heaven forbid, the outcome, I'd do it myself right from our front yard there in Dunkirk. Now, during one such broadcast of mine, on one rare, very rare occasion of an imaginary Notre Dame game—it was close to halftime and believe it or not they were behind 14 to 7 and man, I'm tellin' you, it was one close game, one for the ages. It was so close I don't even recall the opponent; it had to be Ohio or Army, though because they always played us tough. I was so worried about Notre Dame that day and my nervousness had to come through that garden hose to the ears of neighborhood listeners. I hoped though that whoever was listening to my front yard broadcast was also as excited about the game as I was.

I was standing in our yard doing the broadcast of that game and I'd love to imitate Bill Stern—perhaps not imitate, but I liked his style. Bill Stern had come from WHAM and was hired by NBC to do their sports; he was actually the first to broadcast a televised sporting event, a baseball game. Bill Stern had a Paul Harvey quality that I tried to incorporate, I suppose. Anyway, during this rare occasion, Notre Dame was behind and there was only a couple of minutes remaining in the first half---Notre Dame was driving the ball and the game clock was ticking down, the crowd was cheering, everyone was biting their fingernails, and then wouldn't you know? My mother would yell out the front door 'Van—time for supper!'

Supper! I couldn't believe mom was calling me in for supper!

As you can imagine, Rob, there was a momentary disruption in the action on the field. I'd stop what I was doing and yell back to mom. 'Mom, the game! I can't come in now; it's close, awful close. The game! The first half is almost over…I'll eat later!' Remember, the only real game was the one that I was shouting into the garden hose.

There'd be another pause in the action after I told Mom that I couldn't come in just then, and immediately I'd get back into game mode right away.

Then Mom would yell back to me, 'Van, call a time out!' I'd yell back, 'Ma, but Notre Dame doesn't have any timeouts left.' So with no timeouts, the clock running down, and Mom on the porch waiting, I had to finally have Johnny Bertelli throw a touchdown pass to tie the game at halftime.

Your mom was your first official timekeeper?

Yes, she was; but after I had Bertelli throw the touchdown, I felt better about going in to eat knowing the game was tied rather than being down by seven. And, of course, after I returned to finish the second half, Notre Dame went on to a great victory.

I remember Mom always trying to lure me in when I was a bit more stubborn than usual. She'd say, 'Van, c'mon in because we're having your favorite.' Yea, my favorite, all right. 'You'll miss out if you don't come in,' she'd say—a thirty-seven cent can of candied Spam.

Candied Spam or Notre Dame—that had to be a difficult choice for you.

Well, Rob, we always have to listen to our mothers, though it may not always be in a timely manner.

But radio, real or imaginary, is what we had for entertainment, I guess—we had family and church, and that was always the most important to everyone in Dunkirk. I had many friends growing up; as a matter of fact as a kid I met this cousin of a friend of mine his name was Bob Werner. Years later we'd live just a few streets from one another and he'd be my stats guy for forty years. But friends, family, and church—that was important. I played basketball and football; I was pretty good at basketball and practiced with the varsity when I was in eighth grade. I swam in Lake Erie...both my grandfathers were fishermen and they drowned in the lake.

We cared about how our neighbors were doing. We had high school sports to keep us busy but radio, real or imaginary was an escape for me and as an only child being raised by a single mother and my grandmother sometimes we didn't have a lot so I used my imagination to give me other things.

My parents were born around the same time you were, Van, and they were most certainly children of the Great Depression—my father, in particular. Honestly, you remind me of him a great deal in your mannerisms and sense of humor. He was born in twenty-one; he, too, was raised by a single mother and was badly injured as a boy—so bad that he, too, carried scars with him the rest of his days. He and his mother, abandoned to poverty, were staggered by the Depression. How did those years affect you and your family?

Van at two or three years of age.

I can't really say I noticed the Depression. I was still young—five, six, and seven when the Depression was at its most fierce; but it didn't feel like those years even touched Dunkirk. Maybe I was too young to recognize being poor. We were poor, I guess, though I don't think we knew it. I don't think someone knows they're poor until someone else points it out to them. Everyone was poor in Dunkirk at the time, anyway, so we didn't really notice it. My mom and grandmother worked all the time providing for me and giving me whatever I needed, so I didn't lack for a thing. Others weren't as fortunate as I was that I know too.

You speak of your father's scars, Rob. When I was a teenager in Dunkirk and later— well, I was in college—but I was in the first of two terrible accidents, when I was a teenager. Both have always impacted me. My back and legs are still affected by those accidents even today all these years later. I was in the hospital the first time for ten weeks and the second time for eleven weeks.

The first time was during the war years. I was working for a company, a canning company—Bedford Products—when I had the first accident. They had the slogan 'we eat what we can and what we can't we can.' They had a clever slogan but they were lousy bosses.

Well, Freddy Bedford and his brother owned this canning company and one summer afternoon I skipped baseball practice to go make some extra money by loading some jelly jars for them. I, along with two other guys, a couple of buddies of mine, went to load these jelly glasses onto a two-and-a-half-ton rack truck.

Freddy Bedford lived across the field from where a big rail yard was, and also from where we had to get these jelly glasses loaded. We go and load these jelly jars, and Freddy had this big dog, and the dog at the end of each day would jump into the cab of a truck and ride home to its owner—this particular day was no different. This dog jumped into the cab of the truck for his ride back to his owner waiting for him at the canning factory.

So my buddies and I finish what we had to do and we go to get into the cab of the truck to ride back to the main plant and there's no room for us—the dog and the driver are taking up all the space. The front seat was full—it was a big dog. 'Where are we going to ride?' I asked the driver, and he said we could just ride on back on one of the fenders. 'It's not far, not far' he said. The tailgate was up because the back was filled with all these jelly jars, so he expected us to ride on the bumper in some way. I said to the driver that we weren't riding in the back because there was not enough room for us, but that there was enough room back there for the dog. The driver just said no. The dog said no in his own way too. My buddies sat on the left fender and I sat on the right fender.

It was more important for the driver to deliver the owner's dog back to him safely than the employees. The driver had no license to drive such a truck, anyway, and the dog was taking up much of the rest of the cab. I asked him to move the dog again and again he said no, and told me that I, we, could ride on the tailgate. 'No,' I said, because there wasn't anything to hold onto back there. He said he was leaving. There was no choice, so I held on to the back and sat on the fender as best I could.

Well, not only didn't he have the proper license, but also he couldn't drive worth a damn either, and he was banging and bouncing all over the road as we headed back to the canning company. I was holding on with my hands the best I could, and had almost no grip with my feet, so his bad driving and my precarious grip made for a bad mix. He was driving like he was nuts, bouncing us around pretty well. We didn't have far to go and I really was holding like nobody's business. We were in sight of Bedford Products and there was this other truck parked alongside of the road that the driver didn't see. This driver took a sharp turn, one far quicker than he should have to avoid a collision. I slid off the fender and my legs were dragged behind the truck. I was holding on with just one arm and he dragged me behind the truck with my leg stuck up in the running board for a good couple of blocks before he finally stopped. My arm was dislocated from holding on to the back as hard as I did. There was a chunk of meat ripped out of my leg and my back was torn all to pieces.

Now, if this wasn't bad enough—he being an unlicensed driver, having to ride hanging onto the back of the truck because of a dog, and a driver who wouldn't slow down to make a decent turn—he didn't stop to take me to the hospital, either. Now the hospital was only a couple of blocks away from where we were. Instead, he asks me where my doctor's office was and takes me there. I had a hard time answering at first; I had to be in some type of shock and I was bleeding everywhere. Pieces of skin were hanging off, my shoulder was dislocated, I felt it, blood was everywhere, and even the better part of my pants was torn off so I was trying to hold them up with the one good arm I had left.

I was in real bad shape—I did manage to tell him who my doctor was and he takes me down there, to his office building and in so doing driving right by the hospital. He was not a bright man. I don't know if he was scared or nervous, but someone needed to make the right decision at that time and I sure wasn't in any position to do that. Instead of taking me to that emergency room, he drops me off at the front door of this doctor's office; the motor of the truck was still running, he wouldn't even get out and help me inside.

Things being what they were on that day, of course the doctor's office was on the second floor. I had to navigate these long stairwells, bleeding all over the place, and holding my pants up with the good hand I had. It was unbelievable and, of course, the doctor wasn't in, but there was a dentist who shared a common waiting room. He had a patient in the chair and one waiting to be seen when I came in, but he took one look at me and it was he that took me to Brooks Memorial Hospital and I'd be in there for nearly eleven weeks. I still have the scars and my arm still bothers me from that day. I was in high school when this happened and I have never been able to lift it completely since that day.

If I had known about lawsuits and such back then it would have been worth a million I'm sure.

Then it wasn't long after that, a year or so perhaps a little more after I had graduated Dunkirk High School, and I was taking a couple of radio and television courses at UB. The week was over and I was running late in catching a Greyhound bus to take me back to Dunkirk. It was pulling away from the dock just as I got there and the driver had to stop to let me on. I paid the driver when I got aboard and grabbed a seat about halfway back. As I got on I noticed, sitting in the back of the bus on that long seat, were three girls. I knew them all, and had dated one of them for a little while. They had just graduated from Bryant and Stratton. I had dated that one, like I said, so I was hoping that the other two would get off somewhere along the way and I'd get a chance to go back and talk to Donna— that was her name, Donna Muldeen. Well, one of the girls did get off in Angola, but the other one did stay on, so I moved on back a few seats to try to talk a little bit to Donna, anyway; we were east of Dunkirk somewhere on route five.

I was in the last double seat and they were sitting in the last seat…that one long seat in the very back of the bus. We were starting to talk and hadn't noticed, but it had started to rain. Well, for some reason this Greyhound bus had bald or near bald tires and when it tried to navigate a sharp curve in the road it swerved and went off the road; it hit the guardrail and rolled over several times. We had just entered a straightaway near the Dunkirk Conference Center. The road was already slick because of an increasing rain, and combined with the bald tires and a bus that was traveling probably faster than it should have because it just flipped over and over going off the road. The bus rammed into a tree and came to a stop on its roof.

There were two people killed on the bus, including one of the girls from Bryant and Stratton, Mary Noble who was sitting right behind me was killed. I had to crawl out along the luggage rack. I was taken back to Brooks Memorial Hospital and it turned that I had broken my back this time, and I was going to be in the hospital for eleven weeks this time. The surgeon Dr. Foss did give me a choice of sorts, he said, 'Van, you broke several vertebrae in your back; now, I can put you in a plastic cast, but you don't want that. The other choice is if you lay perfectly flat, *don't do anything, lay perfectly flat, all should be fine—well, I chose the latter, of course, but I did have to do everything from a perfectly flat position for ten weeks. I mean everything.*

How old were you when all this happened?

I was in high school at Dunkirk and was late in my junior year or early in my senior year when I had that first accident, and was twenty, I think, when the bus accident occurred.

So, that would put both accidents between nineteen forty-five and nineteen forty-seven or forty-eight, at the latest correct? When we met a couple of years ago for the first time up in the press box, you were doing some stretching exercises and mentioned it was because of a couple boyhood accidents. I take it these were the accidents?

The years sound about right; those accidents have affected me all my years—but I was lucky; people died that day. I'm still here.

After the first accident, I still played ball in high school. My football coach was Karl Hoeppner, but the second accident took a lot out of me. It ruined my sports as far as playing. I turned my attention to being a coach or athletic director, but I still had difficulties but who wouldn't after recovering from a broken back. I did keep playing basketball and baseball after the first accident and even a little basketball at Fredonia State. I liked basketball a lot and usually was good enough to be a starting guard for St. Mary's and even practiced with the varsity and was good enough to play with the varsity, but after I broke my back I couldn't play anymore.

I was quite good at basketball. Even in the eighth grade, I played with the varsity; I went to St. Mary's the first two years, nineteen forty and forty-one or so, and it was at the outbreak of the war and my coach was drafted into the army. I was real close to him and his leaving bothered me a great deal. A coach at Dunkirk High School encouraged me to come over to that school and finish up my last two years; well, since my coach, my dear friend at St. Mary's, was off to the army, I went and finished up my schooling at Dunkirk High School. I have to say something else about my coach at St. Mary's, he was like a father to me—one time he took me down to New York City; I was twelve, I think. We went down to New York City to see the N.I.T. that year; we saw the final between West Virginia and Western Kentucky at Madison Square Garden—it was a great adventure—he came back safely from the war and we stayed great friends.

*N.I.T is the National Invitational Tournament, the only tournament prior to the advent of the N.C.A.A. In 1942, West Virginia was seeded last going into New York City and led by Rudy Baric; they advanced to the championship game, where they defeated Western Kentucky 47–45. It would be West Virginia's last N.I.T until 2007.

"'Tiny' the num-num man."

Rob as a boy it was a tremendous experience seeing New York City and as we've talked about I had the opportunity to work there later on after joining WBEN but chose to stay in Western New York. As you can imagine small stations have a life of their own and you know a lot of strange things happen at a 500-watt station. I need to tell you about this fellow I worked with many, many years ago at WFCB named "Tiny" Hamrick…he was a graduate of the University of Chicago a very prestigious school. He had a double degree in broadcasting and journalism. He was a great guy…one of the best…fun to work with…kindhearted… decent…generous, so on and so forth, but he was the biggest guy I'd ever known. He had to top the scales at four hundred and fifty pounds and his wife my God she was a bird couldn't have weighed a hundred pounds. What a pair they were walking down the street. But "Tiny" dressed impeccably despite being enormous, he wore beautiful sport coats with white Oxford shirts with ties…cuff links the whole nine yards. I had no idea where he ever went to get his shirts. I secretly think that he had Achmed the tent maker as hiss own personal tailor.

Again don't get me wrong "Tiny" was a great guy and a friend and when we worked together he was I read his commercials for him during the week because he did the 9, the noon and the six o'clock newscasts. "Tiny" was News Director and also Program Director at the time and after he finished his stint he went back to his boarding house in Dunkirk where he stayed through the week. His landlady always had a big plate of cookies for him…they'd be waiting on him everyday to return from the station to the boarding house.

"Tiny" was real good friends with the Num Num potato chip salesman and the salesman would come by the radio station every week and leave a big can…a five pound can of Num Num potato chips for "Tiny" who of course had no trouble in disposing of them. Now in our booths we had these wire chairs and "Tiny" hung over all sides of them and he would go through about a chair a week…you know they'd just break them down. He had worked at a station in Buffalo that was on the ground floor but many of the stations were on the upper floors and you would have to use elevators to get to work and because of his weight these companies…these stations were afraid to take a chance on him. They wouldn't hire him

because what would happen if he died on an upper floor…how would they ever get him out…put him in a sling and lift him out the window down the side of the Statler Hilton?

This one time a friend and mine were going to drive to Buffalo to buy ski equipment and we took "Tiny" with us. We had to get him into this Chevrolet hardtop it was a nice enough little car but we had to put "Tiny" in the back seat…we could barely get him in there…it was a two door too. We did manage to get him in there and started up the road toward Buffalo and of course in mere minutes we had a flat tire with him back in the back seat…we had no spare of course so luckily there was a station within walking distance…not to far away…so we went and got the tire fixed and when we returned back from the station "Tiny" had shifted his weight in the back seat and what a mess we had then trying to change the tire I tell you.

There was this other incident with "Tiny"…he be doing his newscasts and I'd be reading his commercials so we would be sitting across from one another with glass separating us. I'd be sitting in the booth doing my show and "Tiny" who was my producer would be sitting across from me with a slab of cheese, a pound of bologna, his can of Num Nums and a knife that was about a foot long. I'd look across to the other booth and all I'd see is "Tiny" slicing his bologna and eating cheese and Num Nums any way one day as we were doing our show there was an incredible amount of interference coming through my headset…loud thundering amount of noise I didn't know what it was until I tossed it to "Tiny" who would then do the news. There was nothing…there was dead air…I looked over and he was sound asleep and snoring just as loud as any four hundred and fifty pound guy could snore…and it was coming through my headset and going out over the airwaves…well I quickly said we are having some technical difficulties and went to a commercial. I went over and woke him up and ran a couple more commercials until he was fully awake. I can say that there is nothing like the sound of a four hundred pound guy snoring with full force into a headset.

It was a fright for a few minutes but he was fine just asleep. I couldn't imagine if he had fallen sick with an overload of some kind…cheese and Num Nums. It was shortly after that I invited "Tiny" over to our house for dinner and Gloria asked me, Van, what are we going to feed him, she was serious too, we can't set five porterhouse steaks in front of him that'd be an insult and even more we can't afford five steaks. Well we bought a pot roast and "Tiny" ate the whole roast instead. He was quite a character, a good man and friend and certainly someone who appreciated his Num Nums and I will never forget the day he fell asleep snoring into the headset.

---

*The Num Num potato chip company was one of the first wholesale manufacturers of potato chips in the nation, located in Cleveland Ohio it was later purchased by the Frito Company.

CHAPTER FOUR

I was a good Catholic boy from Dunkirk, so Notre Dame never lost a game.
We especially beat the hell out of Army every time.

I think it's clear that if Van had not had access to radio during his early years, primarily the mid-'30s, that he may not have developed an interest in the medium. It is also fair to say that if he'd not developed the interest in the medium, that Van may not have tried to fashion his work after the great Bill Stern. If not for Bill Stern, Van may not have mastered his craft. And if not for the Fighting Irish of Notre Dame and the broadcast of their football games, Van's craft, his gift, and the game we all love, football, may never have met.

Notre Dame should be credited for giving to the world many things: astronauts, numerous congressmen and political figures, two presidents—though be it from Panama and El Salvador—and, of course, Phil Donahue. And on the football field they have most certainly produced some of the all-times great coaches and players, as we have already mentioned. But even some sixty and seventy years later, when historians speak of Notre Dame's great football days, they inevitability make their way back to the days of Knute Rockne. But Notre Dame made Van's imagination blossom.

The year—once again—was 1927, and fans of Notre Dame weren't expecting a great team to take to the field that year, but they were looking forward to another *good* season at the very least. That year they would face only three teams they'd refer to as quality teams: Minnesota, Army, and the University of Southern California; but Navy was also on the schedule and was always the biggest game, regardless of won-loss records.

The Notre Dame season began with Knute Rockne being cautious, as he did not reveal his hand early on in the season; perhaps he felt minimal effort was needed, as they easily outscored their opponents 48-7 in the first two games of the year. The scouts for Naval Academy had no idea of what to expect, as they were next on Rockne's schedule; they, too, fell by 19-6. However, November would find a different set of obstacles, as two rough games awaited them. On November 5, 1927, the game against the Minnesota team of Bronislau "Bronko" Nagurski resulted in a 7-7 tie, and the following week they were shut out by Army. These were two tough weeks for Notre Dame.

Not happy with the efforts of his starters on the fifth and the twelfth, on November 19 1927, Rockne played only his second stringers and watched as they took their frustrations out on Drake 32-0. *That* rout that shut out was a reward for many after the losses of the previous two weeks. It was a relief of sorts for the frustrated fans across the country. Perhaps, too, that shut out of Drake was an early birthday present for just three days later on November 22, 1927 Van Miller was born.

The winning streak for the Irish began three days before I was born and, as far as I'm concerned, they haven't lost a game n eighty years. Notre Dame has always been my team—from Angelo Bertelli and Johnny Lujack, to the Four Horseman of earlier years. They have had some tough years, lately, but they will turn it around.

When Charlie Weiss took the job as the head coach of Notre Dame a couple of years ago, he came over from the pro game—the New England Patriots to major college football. It was a big difference. It's a big move if a coach goes from the college level to the pros or the other way; it's expected that when a college coach goes to the pros that this is the way things happen, not necessarily vice versa. Being a great college coach doesn't mean they will be successful on the pro level. Remember John McKay in the seventies? He won four national titles with USC; he was O.J.'s college coach, but when he went over to the pro game, it was a tough move. He coached Tampa Bay their first years in the league. That first season they didn't win one game. So when Charlie Weiss comes to Notre Dame after winning Super Bowls, it was expected that he'd have quick—immediate—success; they will turn things around, though, I'm sure of that.

Yea, you're right. If I remember correctly, Tampa Bay under McKay went 0-12 the following season too, before finally winning the first game in team history.

I think so, Rob. Tampa Bay stunk for almost two years. They were dreadful. The general conception is that a college coach will go to the professional game and not the other way around. There are college coaches who have succeeded at the college level but who bombed went they went to a pro team; Pete Carroll and Steve Spurrier are two that come to mind right away. Now when Charlie Weiss going to the college game from the Patriots, who had won a couple of Super Bowls expectations was high that he could instantly turn things around. The donors certainly believed that. It wasn't so; they have struggled. They'll turn things around, though. But without exception, the greatest era at Notre Dame was that of Knute Rockne, and the fabled Four Horsemen. I was only three when Rockne finished coaching but he was already history.

It might be hard to say, but do you think *that* era may have been one of the best for college football?

Well, it was certainly a historical one. Great names and players and all those great games and for me it was made real by listening to the radio. What changed everything though was television. Now I believe that every era has the possibility of being a great one. Radio made the college game—college football—a more national sport, because after all, if it weren't for radio, I'd have never been exposed to the college game. And it was the college game that got me excited about football and introduced me to broadcasting. The excitement of the broadcast really got me interested in football and in broadcasting itself. Football is just a great game, and every era, in its own way, is a great era, whether it be college or at the professional level. Fans of today, years from now, will look back and say this era was the best for the college game, professional.

The definition of greatness, then, is all in context to the era in which someone experiences the event?

Well, yes. I listened to the teams of Angelo Bertelli, Frank Dancewicz and Johnny Lujack; I see them as some of the best to have ever played the sport. A young fan today will say something else, because they only see the modern game—they have nothing else to compare it to until they have experienced a few seasons.

I'd like for us to back up just a little. You were born in nineteen twenty-seven?

Van's baby picture.

Yes, November twenty-second, nineteen twenty-seven; it would be the same day of the month when John Kennedy was assassinated, and as a matter of fact I was on the air that day, on my birthday. I turned 36 that day. What a time it was; it was my birthday in nineteen sixty-three when I had to deliver the news to everyone that President Kennedy had just been assassinated in Dallas.

You were, are, an only child?

I have stepsiblings—brothers and sisters—but I was an only child growing up. I think I was only a couple months old when my mother had this baby picture done.

Van, I know I have asked some of these questions over and over, but here were go, just one more time for redundancy's sake. My parents were born in the twenties, as well, my mother in twenty-four and my father in nineteen twenty-one. He, too, was an only child raised by his mother during the Depression era. Though my dad never talked about the Depression, I always felt that it had to be a time that he *didn't* want to talk about. You had mentioned earlier on that the Great Depression didn't tremendously impact you?

Well, like I said, the Depression just seemed to pass my family and me by. We were poor, all of our neighbors were poor, but it didn't seem that way. We just lived our lives day to day. You have to understand that my mother was an absolute iron lady; and she, along with my grandmother, Rose Vanderweel, raised me. The name Vanderweel is where I get the name Van. I had no father, so to speak; my father abandoned me as a babe in arms. He left me to the care of my mother and grandmother. My dad was a welder and worked in thirty states all over the country. He'd send me a Christmas present every couple of years and a birthday gift or card— but never any money for us. He came into my life again when I was twelve or thirteen; he had remarried and had other children, but he left my mother and me shortly after I was born.

My mother and grandmother raised me without any help from him. My mother's family lived down by Lake Erie, and my first grandfather was very young, and he left my grandmother without any money, no insurance, nothing, too. This made her, as an older sibling, charged with helping to raise the younger brothers and sisters; this made her grow into a strong woman. Understand, Rob, there was no social security or other state welfare programs at the time, so she, my mother's mother, had to go off and work as a domestic to bring home the stale, nasty bread just to feed her family. My mother was just three years old and she had younger siblings besides her, as well, so she had a very difficult childhood. This was around nineteen hundred or nineteen ten, but they grew up and my mother grew strong. My mother got a job working for a lawyer; then she worked for a bank, the Dunkirk Savings and Loan. They wanted her to be the secretary, but she didn't want all the responsibility. The woman was absolutely incredible; she put the worms on the hook for me, she played catch with me, she was my 'father' for all practical purposes.

What is your mother's name?

Esther Vanderweel. She was amazing. She and my grandmother made sure I never went without.

Van's mother, Esther.

My mother and grandmother would work all the time. I would eat lettuce sandwiches with mayonnaise and I'd walk to school during all kinds of weather, as you can imagine— Dunkirk in the winter. I'd walk to St. Mary's and later to Dunkirk High School. It's what they did for me that really made me want to stay in the area and not take other offers in bigger markets. I didn't want to leave them.

When I was young—old enough to work and help the family—I worked picking berries, and one summer I even worked for the board of education painting. Now I was not a skilled painter that I can tell you and this one summer I fell off a platform while painting and spilt paint all over a hardwood floor…so that job abruptly ended, as the board of education and I simultaneously realized that painting wasn't a strong suit of mine. I also worked for the highway department for a time. I worked one summer, a couple of summers, maybe, as a caddy at the Shorewood Country Club, making a nickel a bag per hole and so I carried two bags for the full eighteen holes and made $1.80. This, too Rob: I worked for a while as a pinsetter at Ping's Bowling Alley. I worked two lanes at a time. I would set the pins in one lane, and then had to quickly set the other lane. I had to be quick or the pins would bounce off me or narrowly miss me and if I weren't quick I'd be hit by a bowling ball.

Van circa 1945.

But again Rob I never really knew I was poor. I enjoyed every aspect of being a kid and growing up in Dunkirk, the Garden Spot of the North. I loved to play basketball. I always loved basketball and when I was in the eighth grade, I practiced and played with the varsity team; but because of the accidents I had, and that I was involved in, I couldn't do what it took to play well. Later, after I was involved in a terrible bus accident, I played a little at Fredonia State, but I couldn't play much, anymore, and when I couldn't go to a game, I'd listen to it on the radio. I listened to a few games and couldn't believe what I was hearing as a player. I think I knew what the announcer was trying to say, but I knew I could say it better, and so I went up to the owner of the station, WFCB, Allie Schmidt, and said, "Now look, the guy you got calling these games doesn't know if the ball is inflated or stuffed. You need me."

Inflated or stuffed—is that what you said?

Yes, that's it; it's true, this guy, the guy calling the games for the Dunkirk station, was terrible. So I talked myself up to the owner. I go up to the station's owner, Allie Schmidt, and said that I would be better at broadcasting and Allies said to me, 'Van, what do you know about calling games? You have no experience whatsoever. Well, I was ready for his answer, I said, 'I beg to differ.' I said, 'I have years of experience calling Notre Dame games and even Joe Louis fights.' Of course, I overlooked telling him that the football games and fights that I was calling were into the end of our garden hose or a wooden spoon. I was working at a small store in Dunkirk at the time. I was working for a couple of stores at the time I started with FCB, and was hoping something else would come my way, and it did. And it was radio. Anyway, Allie hired me, and my career in radio had begun there at WFCB Fredonia – Dunkirk.

The owner, Allie, said he'd pay me ten dollars a game for three games at first, to see how I would do, and you know what he paid me? Seven dollars a game, and as far as I'm concerned, he still owes me nine dollars—more than that when you add in interest. But kidding, Allie hired me and WFCB was where I started.

---

*Note: WFCB first went on the air in 1949 and kept those call letters until 1957. Now it is known as WDOE, the call letters standing for Dunkirk On the Erie.

Let's go back to the Great Depression for a couple of minutes. During the Depression, there wasn't much money, of course, and when I was nine or ten it was right in the middle of it, and when it was over I was just becoming a teenager. So, I can't say I was impacted by it. I was starting school in thirty-two, thirty-three, but Mom and my grandmother did the best they could and I never went without. So probably because of them I didn't realize we were poor. Rob, your parents' families and mine were probably alike in some ways, or anyone growing up at that time; we didn't know we were poor, we just were. We lived day to day. It was probably only the rich or the better off during those days that had any idea that they were poor. They were the ones who knew that things were tough.

Sure, that I do understand; if a person is poor, they may not always realize things are tough. But if someone has something to lose and looses it, that's when they see the difference in life.

Dunkirk was small, then, during the Depression; it's still small. There wasn't much to do in Dunkirk, so we played as all kids do. Fished, and I swam in Lake Erie, but I enjoyed listening to the radio, too, and especially the broadcasts of the Notre Dame Football games. I loved to pretend that I was calling a great game—Notre Dame against Ohio State, Michigan, or Amy. Kids' minds run off a thousand different directions—mine did. Everyone pretending to be this, or that, or the other as kids have done for hundreds of years. I pretended being a radio broadcaster. I wanted to be the Bill Stern of Dunkirk. I think that's probably what some neighbors thought. I had to be seven years old, probably younger, when I remember first listening to the CBS broadcasts of the Notre Dame football games. Their broadcast team of Ted Husing and Les Quailey were great, and I did try to learn from them, too, but it was Bill Stern who I'd come to really admire.

Van, looking quite dapper; his hair parted and ready for a front-yard broadcast.

Being well prepared, Van, I did do a little research on Bill Stern. You chose one of the best to emulate, or to be a fan of, so to speak. Bill Stern began his career, from what I've been able to discover, there in Rochester at WHAM. He was one of the first, if not *the* first, to broadcast the telecast of a major league baseball game and he played himself in the movie *The Pride of The Yankees: The Lou Gehrig Story* with Gary Cooper.

That's right; he played himself in a couple of movies, he even as a star of the Hollywood Walk of Fame. Your wife has kept you busy, I see. We kids all dreamed and pretended and perhaps poor kids might daydream just a bit more. I guess I dreamt of being a broadcaster. When you were six or seven, Rob, you dreamt of being something, right?

I did. I wanted to be a cowboy, a hero riding into town to save Miss Kitty from *Gunsmoke*.

A cowboy? You wanted to be a cowboy?

Yea, Van. I wanted to be a cowboy, but the demand for a seven-year-old, nearsighted, overweight cowboy in 1970 wasn't real high at the time. So I moved on from that thought. But you kept plugging away at your trade, your craft.

I kept plugging away. I loved it from those early days on. I loved to hear the broadcasts. I kept entertaining the neighborhood and always practiced calling games and interviewing people. I imagine I got on some folks' nerves. I don't know how many times I called the game of the century in 1935 between Notre Dame and Ohio State University. It didn't matter, Notre Dame always won.

Rob, like all kids, our imaginations were all we needed to have a good time with, and I remember that I'd take Mom's hand eggbeater—the old type of eggbeater—and hold the beaters end up to my mouth and pretend to call a Notre Dame football game; that's where it all started. Right next to our radio in our living room or the front yard of our Dunkirk home; I called every game I ever heard. If God forbid Notre Dame actually lost my rebroadcast would have a more favorable outcome.

It was fun all over Dunkirk; it's my hometown and it's why I'm so proud of it. It has never been too big and, in my opinion, it's a tremendous place to be a kid. From the first time I started to work at WFCB it was fun. I enjoyed every game I called and everything I ever did in radio, and getting paid for doing what I loved was nice, too—making a living at it—it was a plus too. And in all the years since, it was always fun. It wasn't a job. I was really having a great time every time I sat behind a microphone. But again if it weren't for my mother and grandmother things may have turned much different. They were great, amazing women, my mother and grandmother.

A note here, I attempted several times through the course of our interviews to explore Van's childhood years. I wanted to see what he saw and experience what he experienced as a boy. I believed that getting to know that side of Van Miller might add something more to this book. However, after just a couple of chats, I knew I would learn no more than what he wanted to share and that by itself was good enough for me.

I could certainly tell by his voice, his eyes, and his body language, what those early years were like for him. Words didn't need to be recorded for that. These may very well have been more difficult years than he led on to, but as he said with tremendous love and affection for his mother and grandmother, despite the Great Depression and regardless of being perceived as poor.

I never lacked for a thing, they saw to it. They sacrificed whatever they had for me. My mother was my 'father,' she put the worm on my hook, she taught me to throw a ball and played catch with me. She was my hero. I was so happy to show her what I had grown into, what I was able to do; she was so proud of her son. It was just a wonderful experience for her to watch her son on television.

"Athena's wild ride."

Rob, before we continue, I have to tell you this story; it's about a young woman named Athena. She was the younger sister of Jimmy Georgeson who married my cousin, Ann. Now, Jimmy was a tremendous help to me during my early years with the Bills—he was my first spotter and helped me with yardage and some basic stats. Anyway, Athena was Jimmy's kid sister, a pretty girl. Well, she comes up to me one time and asks me if she could borrow my car so she could take her driver's test. She had turned an age, sixteen, where she had her permit, so she could take her driver's test. Well, her father had taken her out twice to practice and when she had put the car up on the curb a couple of times he told her 'no more lessons from me; it's too dangerous.' So Athena comes to me because I was always sponging dinner, so I was always at her house. I told her, 'Well, sure you can borrow my car.' I had dined at their expense often enough, so the least I could do was to let her borrow my car.

So, the day came and her parents dropped her off at our house. My car was in the drive-way and she said to me, 'Van, I know how to back up.' I said, 'Athena, why don't you let me back the car up.' She was persistent and said, 'No, no, please let me back it up.' So I said, 'Well, okay,' and she backed it up right over my dog, my cocker spaniel. Someone asked me later if my dog was mad, and I said, 'Well, he wasn't real pleased.' I don't think he was too terribly pleased at all, but we never got the chance to ask him. But what the hell.

I gave Athena a few driving lessons and she said she was ready to take her driver's test. I said, 'Athena, you need some more help, you need some more lessons, you need to learn to parallel park better...' 'No, no,' she said she would do a better job the day of the test. So anyway, she went and made an appointment for her driver's test in my car and we go down to the park and meet the guy who was going to administer the test. I move to the backseat and the examiner gets into the passenger seat; and Athena gets behind the wheel. Athena pulled out on to the road and began to jerk and jerk the car down the street, and driving over one curb after another along the way. By now, I was lying on the floor of the backseat, because I figured it was the best place to be. She was asked to parallel park next, and she hit the car both in front and in back of her, and with some force, too, they weren't just taps, I tell you. So, that didn't work out too well either. I could tell that the instructor was getting worried about this time—he was very concerned—and when she started banging the other cars, that's when I laid down on the floor in the backseat to pray the Rosary as she started down the road to the next corner.

She pulled away from the curb, drove down the road, and she was asked to pull into parking lot. And no sooner had the instructor asked the question than she careened around the corner, over another curb and ran the car, my car into a store, breaking its plate glass window, and without taking a breath Athena turns to the instructor and says, 'Well, I guess I'm not going to pass my test.' And the instructors says, 'You're damn right, you're not!' So she says, 'Well, that's okay. I'll go practice a couple more days and make another appointment for next week with you.' And he said, 'Wait a minute! Hold on just one minute!' The instructor said. 'Now look, I'm going to give you your license, but don't you tell anyone where you got it. I don't want to ever see you again.' He gave Athena her license and she goes home and showed her father her license and asks him for a new car. He said, 'Wow, you passed your test, you got your license. Well, let me see how your driving is.' And so she takes her father out and up and over curb after curb and banging this and crashing into that and he said, fine, 'I will give you the car that you want, but there is one condition; for a while I want you to drive wearing a football helmet, because you are terrible.' So for a good while, if you were in Dunkirk, you'd see little Athena driving her car around town wearing a football helmet. As the years have passed the football helmet was set aside accept during some of the more troubling snowy months.

***

I will beat this into the ground Rob, when I was small, two or three, my father was gone but I never lacked for anything. I was always happy and I never knew things were hard.

As I pointed out earlier in this book, all things, all events, happen at a certain time and in a certain way to achieve a certain outcome—an outcome destined to be achieved. We can say—I think, with no uncertainty—that if not for radio, there may have never been a Van Miller in most of our lives. I learned from Van that if not for the love and dedication of his mother and grandmother, the person whom all of us have come to love and affectionately call Uncle Van would never have been. This, of course, is mere speculation on my part, but Van's life could very well have taken a different course, and not that of radio.

When I began to format these early chapters, I wanted to better understand what Van meant by the words *special moments*, the words I had remembered from our first meeting at that Jets game a couple of years ago. I can't say the answer is still clear, but now as Van and I begin to draw to a close our interviews, I may have a sense as to what those moments were, without him ever having to utter a word.

Those *special moments* weren't football related, not all of them. Certainly some understandably are, but not all. They weren't the most important. His face showed all that needed to be said when the longtime voice of the Buffalo Bills had difficulty perhaps putting some memories in words.

It was there in our West Sixth Street home in Dunkirk that I really took solace, comfort, and enjoyment, in a sport that I loved from the first moments I ever heard a game being broadcast. It's what I knew best—sports. I recall my mother one time admiring my blow-by-blow replay of a Joe Louis fight into our garden hose; from those days of making her smile and laugh to having her travel with us to Bills games I was tremendously proud to have her see it.

Her son has done well.
Van nodded.

Yes. I think she was proud of me and it gave me pleasure seeing her pride in me, I have to admit that. I remember how excited she was as I purchased the first television she ever had and I was able to do a lot for her because of the work I was doing and it made me feel good knowing all she had sacrificed for me

His mother, after remarrying, once told a friend that she remembers Van doing these "living room" broadcasts when he was only six years old, both inside and outside the house, and while riding in the family car he began to hone his craft. "He was a master and he was so fun to watch," she'd often say.

Those pretend games were fun and Bill Stern was a terrific broadcaster; I learned many things from listening to him. It's he whom I tried to imitate, so to speak, but I wanted my own style, too. I'm sure when my poor Stern-like impression came out we had neighbors all over Dunkirk who'd scratch their heads, hoping that 'Bill Stern' would go away.

Or that he at least goes in for some syrup heavy candied Spam.

Yea, I believe that some of our neighbors were hoping that their neighborhood 'Bill Stern' would at least go in for a dinner of candied Spam after they had spent hours listening to me. But it was Mom and my grandmother is why I stayed here in this area. I had all sorts of opportunities, offers to move up to bigger markets—New York City and to all three networks, ABC, NBC, and CBS. I told my mom that she could come with us, that I'd move her there. She said no. Dunkirk was her home. So she stayed and I stayed. She remembered that candied Spam, too, and, of course the garden hose and wooden spoons. Many of the neighbors could probably tell horror stories of their own when it came to hearing me over and over.

In one of the early interviews, I read your mom used the words "hone your craft." Let's talk about that a little, about some of your early days. You attended St. Mary's School your freshman and sophomore years, and then transferred to Dunkirk High School to finish up your schooling. When did you begin to hone your craft?

Yes, sir. Then I took some classes at UB and eventually attended Fredonia State. I wanted to be closer to my family, to the Dunkirk area. Later, I would go to Syracuse University, because they did have a communications program that suited me.

During a 2008 interview with *The Observer*, you said, "You can't beat Chautauqua County. God was born there, you know. Dunkirk is my favorite spot." Despite furthering your education and traveling some you were always drawn back to Dunkirk?

Oh, sure. It's the garden spot of the north, Rob; you and your bride really do have to go see it up close if you haven't. I was raised there. It was a great town to grow up in and to be a kid. I'd used to swim in Lake Erie. I am very proud to call Dunkirk my hometown.

Dunkirk is where my friends were. It's where my mother and grandmother were. It's where I played as a kid. I have to tell you, Rob, I absolutely loved basketball and thought that I was good enough to play at the college level, and I was. I played college basketball there at Fredonia State.

Those two accidents, though, ended my playing days for good. Then I thought of being a coach or athletic director, but my physical condition was such that I couldn't do that, either. The accidents had taken too much out of me. Then in nineteen fifty Allie Schmidt gave me my first job in radio there at WFCB.

I read in later interviews that Allie had said you were what they needed…you had come along at just the right time. Professionally, career wise, it was there at WFCB where you began to find your niche.

Yes, I guess Allie was right; I found it, my niche, my calling there at WFCB. After I broadcast my first game he—Allie—comes up to me and says, 'Van, I didn't realize you had that kind of talent,' and there I was, I had someone tell me that I could do it. After that he always spoke highly of me and said that I was the best that he had ever heard. I worked for WFCB for several months before I was drafted. I did have a short stint in the Army during the Korean War. Uncle Sam had me for a little while, but again, because of my injuries from the accidents, my time in the Army was shortened to about four or five months. They wanted to send me overseas to be part of the Armed Services Radio Network, but I received a medical discharge instead and returned to Dunkirk.

Van, on the right, in the Army, circa 1950.

I am guessing at the years, as fifty-one or fifty-two, when you returned from the army. You began to take classes and Fredonia State, did anything special happen for you there? Other than playing basketball and pursuing your studies in communication, that is.

Oh, sure; one particular baton twirler fascinated me; this young lady could perform magic with a baton—a young, beautiful woman named Gloria Chaiko. I was mesmerized, and this year we are celebrating our fifty-second year of marriage. No, fifty-five years…

"It's been fifty-seven years, Van," Gloria reminded him.

Van at Fredonia State.

Yea, fifty-seven years, that's it. Oh my, it's been that long? And buddy, I have to say, that those fifty-seven years have been five of the happiest years I've ever had. But maybe I should move on before I get into trouble. Yes, I did play basketball but Gloria was an outstanding baton-twirler; she performed at Madison Square Garden and at the Polo Grounds. She was tremendous, I tell you. There was this one time when we had Calvin Murphy over one night to our house for dinner. Calvin Murphy, of course, had all those tremendous years at Niagara University and then went on to the NBA and all those fantastic years with the Houston Rockets. Anyway, we had him over one night and he said he wanted to learn to baton twirl, so Gloria sends him out to our driveway and then she comes carrying two batons that were on fire. Well, Calvin backed off when he seen the fire, but I can tell you those two almost burned the house down. Calvin didn't want his hands burned I imagine, good thing, he's one of the best ever to play in the NBA.

Now your question was about WFCB?

Yes, sir, it was there where you began to hone your craft, using your mother's words. Correct?

Yes, I started doing those first few high school basketball games and quickly moved to doing a three-hour-a-day, six-day-a-week morning show; and then became sports director and eventually program director. I'd stay at FCB for about five years, minus time out for the short Army hitch. Gloria and I were married. It was June thirteen, nineteen fifty-three. It was a Saturday, a beautiful day. The birds were singing, rainbows were everywhere that day. In brief I left to take a job at a Niagara radio station. That was short lived. And in March of nineteen fifty-five, I got the job I hoped for and moved over to WBEN. WBEN would lead to television and WBEN gave me greater exposure in Buffalo and that exposure I imagine created a fan base. Ralph Wilson saw that a known local entity such as I was would be best when it came to the hiring of a Bills play-by-play man in 1960.

CHAPTER FIVE

Rob I was determined to get the job broadcasting those basketball games so I went up to the owner of this station and tell him...look buddy the guy you got callin' your games now doesn't know if the ball is inflated or stuffed...you need me.

Though, according to Van, Allie Schmidt may still owe him $9 for those very first couple of basketball games he called, and though he was at first very reluctant to give Van a job Allie Schmidt would say that Van Miller was what the station needed.

He came along at just the right time. We really did need him. Many have said that if it weren't for WFCB and local radio right there in Dunkirk we may never had the voice of the Bills. Van Miller was the best play-by-play guy I ever heard. I don't know where the station may have been without him in those early days.

Though I may have for brevity sake paraphrased Allie Schmidt it was clear from decade old interviews and recollections that WFCB truly needed Van.

And boy Rob did they need me after awhile I wasn't sure what I got myself into because all I was doing was working. Have I told you about my longest day?

No sir, but my ears are anxious.

I was always up early anyway so I was up at 4 a.m. in the morning...as apposed to 4 a.m. in the evening. I was down the road and into the studio by 5 a.m. At this time I was *making $30.00 a week and working a six day week but I was getting talent fees too so that helped a little.*

So I was up and in the studio by 5 a.m. I would pull the records that I wanted to use on my show the 'Van the Morning Man' and I would do that show including the commercials breaks. I would do that from 6 a.m. until 9 a.m. So I did my three-hour morning show, playing my own records and at 9:00 a.m. I did a five-minute newscast.

And at 9:15 I did a show called Relay Quiz, which was a thirty-minute quiz show. I did that show six days a week and that lasted from 9:15 to 9:45 and in that show we would pyramid the prizes. I would call a number from the local phone book and ask her a question about something that we had been discussing and if she didn't know the answer I would ask her for the number of one of her neighbors and I'd call them. I would ask them the same question and whoever won would win something from a wide array of prizes we had. We would give away tiepins, cuff links or a couple of gallons of paint from Service Hardware there on Central Avenue.

The Relay Quiz show went on for a half hour and after that ended from 10:00 to 11:00 a.m. I did a swap shop called The Farmers Exchange where I'd talk for a solid hour about things people wanted to sell or swap dogs, cats or even old cars. I remember this one guy called up once and he was a retired traveling salesman, and he must have purloined Salt and Pepper Shakers from every restaurant and hotel that he had ever stayed. He had written me a little card to me and said Van I have a hundred pair of Salt and Pepper Shakers to sell. I suggested he first call the U.S Army because they might have use of that many pair but I doubted anyone in Dunkirk had a tremendous need for a hundred pair of Salt and Pepper Shakers…anyway I did that show…The Farmers Exchange for an hour and I tell you I talked to all kinds of folks who wanted to buy and sell just about everything. If you want to hear some interesting radio try to find one of those shows.

And after I finished The Farmers Exchange I did the noon news show on WFCB and that lasted about fifteen minutes to 12:15. After that I went right into doing The Polish Program with John Dumichtki I played his Polish records and he read the announcements in Polish and I would read them in English. That went on for an hour I think and after The Polish Program I'd race home and shave, shower, shampoo and race over to the diner for a sandwich and return back to the station to write The Koch's Brewery Sports Review…Koch's was the Dunkirk brewery. They had some of the highest alcohol content beer of anywhere in the country…anyway I'd write their fifteen minute sports review. After I did the sports review I'd go up to Floral Hall where they had professional wrestling on Saturday afternoon and so I would do professional wrestling. I was the ring announcer and I would also broadcast the wrestling on radio for an hour and a half.

This was all the same day?

Yes on every Saturday.

They had professional wrestling in Dunkirk? What matches did you call...do you remember?

Oh God yes I also did professional wrestling shows from Gowanda and the Little Valley Fairgrounds too. Now at that time Suni War Cloud had a long winning streak going on and he was a major draw everywhere he wrestled. They paid me $10 to be the ring announcer...you know...time of the fall 8 minutes 22 seconds. I remember Suni was being billed as a protégé of Jim Thorpe...both being Indian and of course he had his famous move the Indian Death Lock.

When the wrestlers came to town it was a big deal. Some said that Dunkirk was an after thought to the bouts in Buffalo but regardless they'd bring Yukon Eric here, they had Lou Thesz, they had Danny McShain they had The Great Togo...they had Farmer Don Marlin and they had Gorgeous George. The promoter was Ed Don George I remember...it may have been him who got me involved with the wrestlers routines and they usually wrestled best two out of three falls that way the promoters didn't have to bring that many wrestlers with them to town Well in one of these bouts Gorgeous George lost the first fall of his match and he was pretty hot. He was mad at the audience...the other wrestler and so he comes over to me and I'm in the middle of my broadcast and puts his big, clammy paw around my neck and on my nice white sports shirt and I looked at him and demanded in no uncertain terms that he pay the cleaning bill...Gorgeous George just looked down at me...called me peasant and flicked me away as if I was a fly.

The following is courtesy of Steel Belt Wrestling:

Few promoters will pass up a hot hand, so the next Monday, August 7, (1950), George lined up a dandy main event of Gorgeous George, still only a few years into his gimmick, against Jumpin' Joe Savoldi, the Notre Dame footballer-turned-wrestler. George was at the start of his run where he'd draw more than

26,000 to Buffalo in a three-week span. Ticket sales were predictably brisk, with Jordan's New Room, the 1950 equivalent of Ticketmaster, taking more than 100 reservations within hours of the announcement. Promo photos of a bloody George dropping a recent match to Lou Thesz probably only hyped the appearance. Tiger Joe Marsh, fresh off silver screen appearances in "Pinky" and "Panic in the Street" was added as a second attraction against (Johnny) Barend.

Again, a crowd of 2,100 packed the (Chautauqua) fairgrounds, only to be disappointed as George evaded one of Savoldi's trademark dropkicks to score a third fall victory. George wore a long blue robe described as his "George Washington" robe, and stopped Savoldi in the first fall with a flying kick and headlock. Savaoldi got the equalizer in just 1:31 before misconnecting and going down to George's leg lock. Interestingly, Howard "Hangman" Cantonwine acted as a bodyguard to George (his daughter was a robe maker to the star), but he was cheered in his match against Kay Bell. Bell captured that match and Barend won a two-out-three falls contest with Marsh.

Truly, Dunkirk was on a roll. For an August 21 card promoter George brought together Marlin and Lord Jan (James) Blears, a regal heel of the day. In delicious promotional material, Blears disclosed his visits to America were merely a sign of appreciation for the World War II era Lend-Lease program. Advance ticket sales for the card were reportedly strong and it was predicted the crowd would top the previous two events.

***

But anyway I'd do shows at the Little Valley Fairground for the matches and I was also the ring announcer there. I would either did pro wrestling after the Koch's Brewery Sports review on a Saturday... brought to you by Koch's Golden Anniversary Beer*...or I'd do a Fredonia State Basketball game...but on this my longest day I did pro wrestling and as soon as that was over I raced over and did a half-hour live music show from The White Inn in Fredonia. When the music show was finished at 11:00 or 11:30 p.m. I'd go down the back roads back to Dunkirk to The Lincoln Inn and we set up there with The Woodcliff Orchestra and a half hour life music show from 12:00 p.m. to 12:30 a.m. so my day started at 4:30 a.m. on a Saturday and ended near 1:00 a.m. the following Sunday morning...I guess Allie really did need me.

*Fred Koch's purchased Metz Brewery circa 1888 and after a fire in the early part of the 20th century it became known as the Lake City Brewery and produced beer and ale until 1920. During prohibition they produced "near beer" and various sodas and after prohibition was repealed they introduced various beers and to celebrate their 50th anniversary they introduced Koch's Golden Anniversary Beer.

***

I guess FCB did need you. After a day like that you would bring home a good $20, $30?

Well a little bit more because I also received talent that but not much more I assure. There is this story too Rob. Have I told you about the day the mailman delivered me to Salamanca?

"Neither rain nor snow nor broken down Pontiac."

Rob this is about the day that history was going to be made in Salamanca. This had to be sometime in the early '50s because I was still driving my first car, that 1941 Pontiac. So the car was already at least ten years old by the time I was driving it around Dunkirk. I was on my way down to Salamanca to broadcast a high school football from there and it was going to be a momentous occasion so I was quite anxious to get down there. I had gone down there a week earlier and told everyone I knew that they should come out to the Salamanca High School Football stadium the following week because something truly historical was going to happen. The radio broadcast of the football game the following week would be the first ever radio broadcast emanating from the town of Salamanca. It was history so I was expressing that point to everyone I was speaking to and really emphasized the fact to the schools administrator.

During that time of my first visit when I was speaking to the administrator I asked him if they could build me a platform of sorts...because there was nothing from which I could do my broadcast. I needed a platform above the top of the bleachers so I could set up my equipment and call the game. I needed a place for a couple of card tables and chairs as well as the basic equipment needed to broadcast.

I remember one time early on when I called a football game and there was no platform so they set me up in one of the end zones on the back of a pickup truck. I could only see out to the fifteen-yard line. But Salamanca...I went there to prepare the way a little better. I spoke to the Superintendent of Schools there and believe me the stadium was sparse, very primitive in ways. They had a small box...press box for a P.A. announcer but there was no room to broadcast from so I am telling the Superintendent this the upcoming high school football game between Fredonia and Salamanca was going to be momentous and I was going to need a place to broadcast from. I guess he was convinced or was becoming excited too so he built a platform so I could place my table and chairs along with my equipment. The day for the game had arrived and a buddy of mine and I placed the chairs and tables along with my broadcast equipment into that first car of mine the 1941 Pontiac.

I drove over through Cherry Creek. Well as things go we broke down about half-way to Salamanca we had blown a radiator. Fortunately there was a garage close so we walked to the garage told them where the car was and I left my buddy Tony Vicanti there with it and I began to hitchhike to Salamanca carrying the tables, folding chairs and my broadcast equipment. It was unbelievable...I had stuff slung over my shoulders and both my arms were full and about a half hour after I started walking along came Charlie Rhodes. Charlie was a square dance caller and we had done many shows with him and we knew each other real well but he was also the rural mailman for that area. He said climb in Van and he gave me a ride to the Salamanca High School to that broadcast. I was stuffed into the back of his mail truck with all our equipment but that's how I arrived to do the first radio broadcast emanating from Salamanca, delivered with the rest of the mail by Charlie Rhodes.

CHAPTER SIX

I think I knew a merger between the AFL/NFL was going to happen after the
New York Giants signed Pete Gogolak, the kicker from the Buffalo Bills.

    You know when the AFL began, when the Bills began to play, the AFL was considered
a league of wash-ups—cast-a ways—but there were some real good ball players right from the
beginning who played with the American Football League. Getting positive press was difficult,
especially in cities where there was a rival NFL team. New York, for example, and out in
California you had both the Rams and the Chargers in the same city, and the Oakland
Raiders were just a stone's throw from the Forty-Niners—so positive press was difficult to get
at first. But, the years went by and the AFL crowds grew in size; positive press stories were
being written and, most importantly, good football was being played.
    Again, there were teams—AFL teams—that came close to folding the Oakland Raid-
ers and Boston Patriots were two of them, now they are two-storied franchises, but as I have
mentioned, if not for the generosity of Ralph Wilson, those teams would have gone under and
that has to be remembered, but anyway, I knew that a league merger was inevitable when Pete
Gogolak, the place-kicker for the Bills—who was making pretty good money at the time, it
was 1964 and 1965, the championship years for the Bills, he went to the NFL. Pete was
from Hungary and he pioneered the soccer-style kicking—Ralph Wilson paid him, I think, at
least I was told that it was decent money for the day for a kicker. Gogolak said 'no' to a pay
raise and played out his option. This made him a restricted free agent and forced the Bills to
match offers from other teams. The New York Giants, who needed a kicker badly, crossed
league lines, so to speak, and signed him to an NFL contract; now, there had always been in
place a gentlemen's agreement between the AFL and NFL, meaning that one league wouldn't
attempt to sign players from the other league. But the Giants needed a kicker badly, and so
therefore they signed Gogolak to a contract; the Bills wouldn't match it and Gogolak would go

on to be the Giants' all-time leading scorer. When that signing happened, I believed a merger was inevitable, because a bidding war started for players. Pete Gogolak, I think, may still hold the record for most consecutive extra points. This was '65, I believe, and in '66, the announcement was made that the merger would take place in seventy.

I remember hearing that after that signing of Gogolak by the New York Giants, that Al Davis called Ralph Wilson and said, we—meaning the AFL—had just won the war, and suddenly college players were being hid in hotel rooms and backroom deals were being made for players from the other league. Promises were made to players for this, that, and everything else, and let's face it, the AFL did win the war when they signed the $400,000 quarterback Joe Namath; he didn't get exactly $400,000, he got $389,000, but the larger figure sold better to the newsman. I'll tell you this too that I had predicted on the air that the AFL might not win the first or the second Super Bowl—it wasn't called the Super Bowl then—but I predicted they would win two out of the first four titles. That was a good prediction, as you know, for in Super Bowl three the Jets beat Baltimore 16–7 and then Kansas City, who had defeated the Bills in what was technically the first AFC Championship game, went on and crushed the Minnesota Vikings and the "Purple People Eaters"—Jim Marshall, Alan Page, and Carl Eller. That Chiefs team under Hank Stram was a great, great team. So my prediction proved to be correct, as the AFL won Super Bowls III and IV.

Like I said, I had heard Al Davis had said to Ralph Wilson that when the Giants signed Gogolak, that the AFL had won the war—and that was true; you know, there was tremendous animosity between the AFL and NFL at the time. There was this one incident where Alex Karras—I think he was with the Lions—they were going out to Denver to play the Broncos and he said 'if we lose to these chumps I'll walk home.' Of course, the Lions go out there to Denver and get beat by the Broncos, but Alex Karras never walked anywhere.

Let me say this too, when Joe Namath gets off the plane for Super Bowl three, he is so spitting mad at all the negatives he had been hearing, at all the disparaging remarks being made by the Colts and by most of the newspapers in the country, so as soon as the Jets get there for the game, Namath never shuts up from the moment the Jets landed, 'We're going to beat them'—the Colts. I guarantee it was his famous prediction. A funny thing here, now Norm Van Brocklin, 'The Dutchman,' comes into the press box and he says to everyone—and I'll never forget this— he says in a very loud voice, 'Joe Namath is about to play in his very first professional football game'—Van Brocklin was a coach with the Vikings at the time, this was about as negative a comment that could be made about the quality of teams and players in the AFL. Well, talk about putting your big Dutch boot in your big Dutch mouth. And, of course, the Jets won and I think it was that game, that one game, that got him, Namath in to the hall of fame. But Joe Namath, he had a great arm; he didn't have to draw back at all, he stood flat-footed and just let it fly. Getting the job at WBEN though did open many professional doors for me but it also allowed Gloria and I to purchase our home and begin our family.

Van, so many people, your peers especially have said that you made it, broadcasting, look so easy.

Van, Gloria, Cathryn, and Van Michael.

Rob I tell this to everyone, especially to my color guys when they first started, it's not rocket science—I watch the ball and you watch everything else. I learned to paint a picture of what is happening for the listener who may have his eyes shut. So I guess I paint with words. The more I learned to do the more I think I made the broadcasts better. I had to learn to listen first. That goes back to Bill Stern I listened to what he was doing and I learned to like and dislike thing that I would listen to and that helped me understand what my listeners might like or dislike.

Backing up just a little when moved to Buffalo I had a short stint at a Niagara Falls radio station, but then came WBEN; that was my big break. I was hired as a summer-replacement, fill-in type and I stayed for forty-three years...I don't think I was ever told that I was hired full time, I just kept showing up for work; or the station would ask me to do one thing, then another, and then something else. But WBEN was the break I was looking for...we settled down and the kids started school and we began to enjoy it all.

As I entered the world of Van Miller one thing, well, several things became quite clear about his relationship to his former profession. He loved doing what he did and according to so many he did make it seem easy.

Rob, if a person enjoys what they are doing, it should be easy; if a person dreads going to work, it makes sense that they are not likely to be happy or to do well at it. If this is the type of person that sits behind a microphone or in front of the camera, their unhappiness will show in their performance. But what I do or did, it's not rocket science.

Van was right. Here is an example from some time ago, when we had asked him to record a television commercial for us relating to a current project we were working on. He graciously agreed. We go up to his home, the sound system is set up, the camera is rolling, and in *one* take, *one unrehearsed take*, and he records a perfect commercial. The rather experienced cameraman who was there was, to say the least, amazed.

I was amazed, too; in my scattered years of media exposure, I had done numerous radio interviews and always made painstaking efforts to rehearse and study every likely question and answer and word emphasis that might dribble across the interview table. Not Van. It was second nature to him. He had been doing it for over fifty years by that time, too; but none-the-less, he had fun doing it and it showed.

"How do you make it look so easy?" the cameraman asked that day.

"It is easy—it's not rocket science," he said.

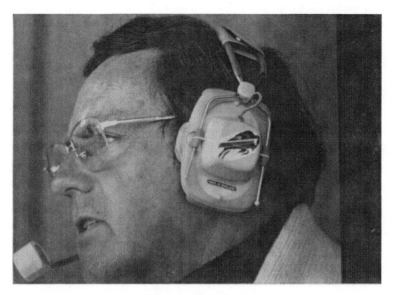

It's not rocket science.

If you like doing what you do, especially in broadcasting, the listeners and the viewers will come. They will know you like what you are doing and they will stick with you and if, of course, you are uncomfortable at doing a broadcast, it's likely you will stink and the listeners may choose something else.

I think we have seen many in the television studio or heard many more in the radio booth struggle in broadcasting a game. One of the most glaring, for me, was watching comedian Dennis Miller try to lighten up a Monday Night Football game. He was a good choice for *Saturday Night Live* but *not* a good idea for broadcasting:

"The punt returner got smacked like Nancy Kerrigan's knee on souvenir pipe night."

Okay, that was a good one, I'll admit. But what about:

"The secondary provides worse coverage than a Guatemalan HMO." Not so good.

The *Monday Night Football* audience soon began to express their discontent, because there were far more bad moments than good ones, and Dennis Miller was soon elsewhere. There are some former athletes who were tremendous on the field, but stank to high heaven in the booth; and in my opinion, the executives believe that a on the field, appeal will attract the listeners or viewers. Their talent was on the field, perhaps; it's not in the booth. I recalled those words as I spoke to Van's former broadcast partner, Greg Brown.

It's not rocket science, nor is it brain surgery; it's just not that complicated. This little bit of advice from Van is what helped me in learning the craft of being a color commentator. In other words, don't try too hard to be good and certainly don't try too hard to be entertaining. The audience—they aren't fools, especially radio audiences; they know a phony when they hear one.

Greg, why so for radio more than television?

Radio, well, I'll say even more so for the Buffalo Bills' radio audience. For a fan to listen to the game on the radio, they are hardcore, dedicated fans; they like what they hear, and they have very likely been listening to that station, that announcer, for years. I know firsthand; and I'm sure so many people have told you that when the Bills game was on, they would turn the volume down on the TV and the volume up on the radio, just to listen to Van doing the game. The radio sports fan is a true-blue, hardcore fan; and I know in Buffalo, the fans they listened because of Van. There were some lean years there for the team, and Van, you know, he was everyone's friend, he was his or her Uncle Van. He was the bright spot for the listeners.

I was coming aboard to fill the chair of the departing Ed Rutkowski. I had done Buffalo Bisons' games for five years, but I was still nervous; I wanted to impress, so on and so forth. Training camp was underway and I was about to call my first game aside Van. It was July of ninety-one and we were to play an exhibition game against the Philadelphia Eagles and we were in England playing at Wembley Stadium. It was a dramatic setting, regardless if it was a preseason game or not. It was one of the first NFL games to be played outside of the United States, as part of the American Bowl series.

Honestly, I don't recall the game much at all. What I do remember is that I did poorly in my 'first at bat,' so to speak. I remember Gale Gilbert was the starting quarterback and the Buffalo media the next day, well, they really basted me over my performance.

I was feeling low down about it all, and Van said something to me that day that I have carried with me throughout my entire career. He said:

Buddy'—he calls everyone buddy—*'as you know by now, buddy,' he said, 'what we are doing is not going to change the world in any way—not one bit. It really doesn't matter when the game is over, it is just a game; it's not rocket science.*

Greg, I added, I have spoken with the former Buffalo Bills' and current color commentator on Bills broadcasts, Mark Kelso, and he has said the same thing: that broadcasting is not splitting the atom, it's not brain surgery, and at the end of the day, it really doesn't matter in the overall revolution of the world.

That's right. I think Van left all of his partners with that. He trained me and I've brought that—what he shared with me—down to the radio booth here in Pittsburgh. I think he trained John Murphy and John likely passed it on to Mark.

I think it's important to add that I was just one of many. Van called Buffalo Bills games for forty-three years, I think, when it was all said and done. He has many partners—Ed, me, Murph—and one year I think the network even tried to add a morning DJ from their rock station to attract a younger demographic. That didn't last too long, I don't think; the network realized that Van was all they needed, and honestly, that's all the listening audience wanted. If they wanted gimmicks or gags, they'd listen to something else on a different station.

A fan knows this: a broadcast, especially a sports broadcast, has to exude excitement even if the game is a dull one. In baseball—I have sat through some dull games, and I am sure Van might say the same thing—but a great broadcaster can't make the games sound dull. Van was brilliant at that, and did that with every call he made; it was natural for him, and those who do not have that skill, I think it shows. If a dull broadcaster is placed in a position where he has to call a dull game, the results will be terrible.

For Van, it was always fun; he enjoyed the practices, the pre-season, the fans. He really loved the fans, and for me it was like I was traveling with Elvis. The fans adored him at home and by fans on the road. I have never seen anything like it, ever.

We'd be in the radio booth at the stadium and, as you know, that's very tiny; there isn't much room in there. And whenever the Bills made a big play or scored a touchdown, he'd jump up on our table or high-five the fans down in front. He'd been doing Bills games for over thirty years by the time I came along, and he was getting along in years by then, too, but he showed his love for the game and the fans and it was infectious. During the bad times—and boy, when the times were good, it was something else.

The latter was shown no clearer than during the comeback game. What an amazing, incredible experience that was. I will never forget. It was late in the second quarter and Warren Moon was having the game of his life. We—the Bills—were down twenty-eight to zero, I think, and I turned to Van. 'Van, this is bad—real bad—it's horrible,' and so on and so forth, I went. I was getting down. I think it was an engineer who might have said,

'Well, it just means that we'll be playing golf a little sooner.' But I'm pretty sure Van said that there was still an entire half to go—he is forever the optimist.

Halftime ended and we all know what began to happen once the third quarter started; Frank Reich came out and immediately threw an interception to Bubba McDowell, who returned it all the way for another Oilers touchdown, and the stadium began to empty like you wouldn't believe. It looked like a high school crowd in 80,000 seats.

Then the Bills scored once, twice—Pete Metzelaars, Don Beebe, Andre Reed—and in very little time the deficit was cut to just four points. The place was going nuts. People began to turn around, heading back to their seats, but they wouldn't let them back in. The Bills scored again, and the cars that were on their way home began to pull over to listen to the game—and it was all because of Van Miller. All the fans that had left the game began one giant tailgate party all throughout Orchard Park, listening to Van call the greatest comeback in NFL history.

It was an incredible honor for me to have worked alongside Van on that day because it was history. I don't think we will ever see anything like that again; it was truly amazing. My time with him was tremendous; it really was the boost that I needed to get my own broadcast career started. He taught me so much, and I hope I listened. Techniques, nuances, pauses and hesitations, delivery—he knew it all. He can and should be ranked with the Harry Carays and Jack Bucks, but I believe Van Miller is the best to ever have sat behind a sports microphone. This, coupled with his love and knowledge of the game, endeared him to fans everywhere, and is what ultimately made him a member of the Pro Football Hall of Fame.

Van with Greg Brown.

*Greg Brown was color commentator alongside Van from 1989–1994 and was with Van during all four Super Bowls. For the last fifteen years, he has been in the radio booth calling Pittsburgh Pirates baseball for Fox Sports Net 104.7 F.M. Greg was replaced as color commentator by John Murphy.

***

Greg really said all that? He's a good guy, and please remind me Rob before the day ends to send a nice reward for his kind words. Speaking of the comeback game have I told you about that day yet?

No, Van; I hoped you might, though. I was one of the few and the proud to have actually seen it on television; it was blacked out up here, but I saw it in Tennessee, where I was living at the time. It was your call of the game that I remember from the NFL post game shows.

Well, everyone knows that the Bills at the low point in the game were behind 35–3; Warren Moon was an absolute machine that day. The Run and Shoot offense was clicking like nothing I remember ever seeing before. It was running perfect and the Oilers and the three receivers they had called the Smurfs—Haywood Jeffries, Ernest Givens, Webster Slaughter, and Curtis Duncan—they were running all over the place. I was down, really down, too. I'm a fan, but when you're a professional broadcaster you make every play right and you give credit to Warren Moon when he makes a great play—you say that it was a great play. It seemed to me that all I was doing was complimenting Warren Moon throughout the entire first half. Well, many fans stayed in their seats through halftime when the Bills were down only 28-3, but when Frank Reich threw that interception at the start of the second half that was returned for a touchdown the stadium began to empty out, everyone was trying to leave the stadium. Fans were disguised as empty seats. Then, within a just a few minutes, they were all trying to get back in, but they weren't letting them back in because—I think—of the alcohol issue. But don't tell anyone I said that.

As you mentioned, Rob, the game wasn't on television, of course, because it wasn't a sellout; so I was the only game in town, Greg and I. And it was—I'd say without any doubt certainly—my greatest broadcast. I think it was certainly the one where the suspense kept building like no other game I had ever done before. The mood of everyone couldn't have been lower than it was at the end of the first half, until of course, when the Oilers returned the interception all the way for a touchdown to get the third quarter started. Then the stadium emptied. But no sooner had the bottom been reached then on that very next kickoff the Oilers hit a squib kick and Frank hit Metzelaars and then Don Beebe caught one and then Andre…and the suspense began to build and build and build. For an announcer, it was incredible. The Bills, in just a few minutes, had closed the deficit to four points, after being down by thirty-two.

It, the excitement was really building; the suspense with Andre Reed scoring three touchdowns, penalties going the Bills' way, short punts, and the Bills defense holding Moon to three and out. It was tremendous. It was a playoff game against the Oilers, it was sudden death, there was no next week and in the game, Rob, remember Jim Kelly went down and Frank Reich had to come in and he saved the day. Much like he did when he quarterbacked Maryland. Frank Reich quarterbacked the greatest comeback in both college and professional football history—people need to remember that about him.

I don't think there will ever be another comeback like that again. We'll never see that again, I don't think. It's like Joe DiMaggio's 56 -game hitting streak—you'll never see that again, at least as far as I'm concerned, it's just out of the realm of believability. Nate Odems was the hammer for the final nail that day; he made the interception, which sent in Steve Christie, and he kicked us into the Super Bowl. His shoe from that game—Steve's shoe—is in the hall of fame in Canton.

Van, do you remember the call on that winning Steve Christie kick?

Sure. Do you want to hear? I have it saved; I'll play it for you. After that game that call was put on everything—it was printed on key chains, bottle openers, BBQ forks —everything. I'm a pain in the ass, aren't I? But that was without any doubt, my greatest broadcast so I want you to hear it.

Van left the room, returned and clicked a recording.

"Here it is…we're looking at a thirty-two-yard field goal and maybe the impossible dream, the impossible comeback by the Bills….Reich puts it down. The kick is on the way and it is good—and the Bills have won it! The Bills have won it! They win it forty-one to thirty-eight. Incredible! What a comeback by the Bills. The fans are pouring onto the field—this place is fandemonium."

I have to be honest with you, when we sat in Van's living room and listened to that call being played, a chill shot through me as if I was watching it all over again.

I got pretty excited, there. You know, I was never a screamer. I can't stand to hear people scream when they're behind the microphone, especially when they are homers. I was never a homer. I hate homers. But on that day maybe I did scream and holler just a little.

I got pretty excited that day. I was never a screamer…I can't stand to hear people scream when they're behind the microphone…especially when they are homers. I was never a homer, I hate homers because they can't be objective but on that day maybe I did scream and holler just a little. Who wouldn't be a screamer? The game was done before the second quarter was over. I thought it was over for sure when we fell behind 35-3, our first touchdown could have been seen as a give me but when the Bills recovered the ensuing kickoff and Frank Reich threw 40 yards to Don Beebe I began to have second thoughts.

Don Beebe

I think every player's recollection of Van is of his personality and his fun-loving attitude. I don't think I ever seen Van in a bad mood. He was just always happy when he was around the guys in the locker room or on game day. He was someone you could always strike up a good conversation with and never have him get bored or certainly vice versa. What made Van; Van was his ability as an announcer to get you excited and when you listen to Van on the radio he was one of those rare guys who got you excited about the game too. Van would share the excitement with the listening audience every time he called a game and he is certainly a Hall of Fame commentator that's for sure.

Those Super Bowl teams, those years in general, it was so fun. We had such a unique group of individuals. We were a fun, close group of guys, we were a family and there were people like Van who were apart of it too…even though he was a member of the media he was just as much a part of the family as any of the players. He traveled with the team and was just one of the most genuine people anyone could ever meet.

I believe he had opportunities to go elsewhere too, he had the talent and track record of success. He could have gone to other, much bigger markets and to work nationally but he stayed here in Buffalo. It was his home Buffalo is where his family and friends were and it's where his memories are.

Let me go back a minute to when Ralph Wilson chose Van to broadcast the Bills games that was kind of Ralph's style. Van may not have had the big town credentials that some of the others may have had but what Ralph wanted in anyone he hired was someone that was trustworthy, and family oriented and Van was that way. If you go down the list of names there was Marv, Bill Polian, John Butler and he, John would get players that would have that quality...it was a prerequisite by the scouting department to get people who were obviously talented but who can get along too. They had to have character and Van was a part of that and it didn't surprise me that Van didn't want to leave for other places and it doesn't surprise me that that is why Ralph hired him when perhaps he could have hired "bigger" names. You can see that so many of those early guys have stayed right there it's the family hometown quality that Van always had.

As far as breathing life into a broadcast Van could do that like no one else like. As I mentioned Van could deliver excitement to the fan and...well let me give you an over view of the most obvious one, the comeback game. We were down 28-3 at halftime and we're just getting ours butts handed to us and my locker was next to Steve Tasker's and I remember looking over at Steve and he asked me where I wanted to play golf that Monday morning. Darryl Talley he was vocal and Frank he was a much more a quite type of guy saying pretty much the same thing but the whole atmosphere was... well they scored 28 on us let's go out and score 28 on them and of course the first thing to happen in the second half was Bubba McDowell gets an interception and returns it all the way and now we're down 35-3 and the only one who was positive was Frank. Frank was just going up and down the sideline pumping everyone up but the place, the stadium, it had emptied out...it was I mean seriously empty.

That day Rob, it really was such a surreal feeling when one minute there was 80,000 people in the stadium and the next minute it felt like there was nobody there. Everything started going our way. There was the bad kick and we scored quick and then I caught a forty-yard touchdown pass and the noise started to get louder and it was weird, the stadium was packed then it was empty and when the middle of the fourth quarter came around it was packed again because people had left or were going home and they had been hearing Van call the game on the radio on their way home. They had heard what was happening and so they turned their cars around and were trying to get back into the game but they weren't letting them back in because of the alcohol issue and so folks started jumping the twelve foot fence and finally they just decided to let everyone back in.

It was so loud and I remember it was so loud. I remember I was standing on the side-line and I can't remember if it was Andre's first or second touchdown but it was so loud that the ground was shaking it felt like an earthquake. I mean I had never in all my days have I been in a stadium that was so deafening loud it was an amazing feeling. I'm a high school coach now and I coach a team in Aurora Illinois and I have never felt that kind of excitement before…even after I left the Bills and I won a Super Bowl with the Packers…I never felt anything like I did that day in Buffalo. The thing is one minute you think you are completely out of it and the next minute you think my gosh we can win this and it happened right before our eyes…it was amazing. I could only imagine how Van was calling it had to be tremendous.

I get ask a lot who I might take as my quarterback…some people are shocked that I say Jim Kelly over Bret Favre. Jim was a great leader and could move the ball at a tremendous clip. Scoring that touchdown that day was memorable because it was a part of the greatest NFL comeback ever. It is important to me to have played that part in Bills history but I have to tell you this too that every guy I have played with that was there in Buffalo for a good times everyone of them would say…if they were asked where would you like to go back to in life if you could everyone one would say to that time in Buffalo it doesn't get any better than there in Buffalo. The people of Buffalo are the brunt of many jokes but during those years they were able to thumb their noses at folks. Buffalo is a tremendous city and the fans there are none better anywhere. There was none better than Van Miller behind the mic. He told the story of the game that made it fun and exciting to everyone and I was blessed to have known him during those tremendous years.

Don Beebe against Cleveland, courtesy of Mike Groll.

* Don Beebe had a nine-year NFL career playing six years in Buffalo. Don played in six Super Bowls winning a title with the Green Bay Packers in 1997. He is the head coach of the Aurora Christian Eagles football team in Aurora Illinois.

***

I wanted to add another view of the comeback game in this section of the book, and it most certainly is a different view. Despite the game being blacked out in the Buffalo area because it wasn't a sellout, it was televised to the rest of the nation. And calling the game for NBC that day was the late Charlie Jones and Todd Christensen, the two-time Super Bowl champion tight end of the Oakland Raiders.

Todd Christensen

Rob to do a playoff game for a broadcast team was the tops…it was it; and Charlie and I were asked to do the Buffalo Bills and the Houston Oilers for NBC. So it was an honor for us to do the game and the game had great promise with Warren Moon with the Run and Shoot versus Jim Kelly and the K-Gun. I was still pretty new to the booth.

First up is did you go immediately from the Raiders to NBC?

Actually the Raiders…let's see. The first year after I was cut, I did a show called American Gladiators and, well, what happened is I was let go during training camp of 1989, and the only thing that I did for work at the time was a show called Up Close with Roy Firestone, and I used to be a contributor to that and then the American Gladiators came up and then football season was close, and that's when NBC hired me. So, I guess you can say I had a year of TV training prior to going into the broadcast booth. I think, or the general assumption was, that I needed to improve my chops, my TV presence, first before going into the broadcast booth. Honestly, I don't think I was given a chance to end my football career the way I wanted to, but that's neither here or there. We had won Super Bowls in 1981 and 1983—in '81 against the Eagles and 1983, Super Bowl XVIII against the Washington Redskins. That game is of course best known for the great reversal in the backfield by Marcus Allen. The first year we beat the Eagles in '81 was the first year a wild card team had won the Super Bowl.

I saw something that intrigued me a little; as a tight end, you had led the league in receptions for a couple of years?

That's correct, I did; what had happened during my era following the seventies, there weren't the great athletes at tight end. Dave Casper—he and Ray Chester of the Colts, I think, were the first two that may have been the first genuine downfield threats playing at tight end, but for the most part, you didn't see that. You might see a five to ten-yard button hook or a short crossing pattern, but never much downfield; and when Don Coryell got to San Diego at the start of the eighties, Kellen Winslow was a phenomenon, because a tight end wasn't supposed to be that big and that fast and that athletic. He was six-six and 250, or what ever he was, and he had great hands and they'd use him in the slot. Then Ozzie Newsome, he was a great quality player with the Browns; he was a match up problem, because he had the speed of a wide receiver, but he was the size of a tight end. And then after that, I came along but I had to wait my turn but I did get my shot.

The Cowboys drafted me and they also cut me and I was picked up by and cut by the Giants, and I had tryouts with the Eagles and Patriots, Bears and Packers, and then I came on the scene about four years in. Now, I do have friends telling me that I should be in the hall of fame, and I did play on championship teams and the previous two tight ends I mentioned did not, and I had more pro bowls than Winslow and Newsome too. They are in Canton and I am not. But I played on a team that had some very high profile teams and, as a result, may have taken a backseat to that. But, for example, in that '83 Super Bowl, Marcus may have gotten the MVP but we were, in fact, a defense driven team; we won that Super Bowl 38-9, if I recall.

We had how many hall of famers on that defense—Howie Long, Ted Hendricks, Mike Haynes, and a couple of others that should be—but I have a couple of claims to fame. I am still the only player in the history of the NFL to have led the league in receiving and play for a Super Bowl champion; I would be disingenuous with you, Rob, if I didn't hope for the chance to go to Canton, but if it doesn't come to fruition, I think I'm secure in the knowledge that I played alongside the best. As a matter of fact, Tom Flores coached us, and he has a claim as a player. Tom had played for the Bills and was released by Buffalo, and when Len Dawson of the Chiefs got hurt—Kansas City brought him in because he could also hold for kicks and, of course, that year he won a ring with Kansas City in Super Bowl three. It wasn't the Super Bowl then, but the AFL-NFL World Championship. The first AFL team to win the title was Kansas City and Flores was on it.

Curious…you wore the number 46; that's not a typical number for a tight end.

It's interesting, the reason I got at the time. As I mentioned, I was cut by a couple of teams and I was drafted out of college as a fullback, because that's the position I played; but I am six-three, so I was too tall to play fullback, and so it was assumed that I'd be moved to tight end. And so when I got to the Raiders, I asked for 44, which was my high school number which nobody had; but the next day the equipment manager says to me, 'No, Al wants you wear forty-six.' So it's a forty because I was a fullback, and it's forty-six because Al wanted me to wear it. And I asked why, and he explained to me that during the seventies, they had a prominent player named Warren Bankston, who had played fullback-tight end, but had excelled on special teams and was a special teams captain. I could assume that was what Al had in mind for me—to be a special teams captain.

Let's go to January 3rd, 1993—the Bills and the Oilers.

That was one of my most memorable days. As a former player, what I remember is if you're Houston, there is no way you can't look at that as a choke. You—the Oilers—were up 35–3, and it's the third quarter, so all that a team has to do is hand the ball off three times and punt because no team will score every time they have the ball, and they're certainly not going to score a touchdown every time they touch the ball, so all that you have to do is run and punt and you're fine with it. For Buffalo, at the point in time, your starting quarterback isn't even playing; Kelly was out, it's the second half you're down by thirty-two points and, well, as a player you say to yourself, 'We're not going to be disgraced here; we're not quitting,' but realistically, in your head, you're elsewhere.

People will say all the right things on the sidelines: 'Yea, we never gave up,' 'we were always in it,' no, they may have said that but it's not what they thought. If any Bills player tells you that when they were down 35–3 they thought they could win it, they'd be lying to you. They would be totally and completely disingenuous with you if they thought they were going to win; but there is something in athletes that says 'I'm here, this is what I do and this is what I get paid to do—there are 80,000 people in the stands and I am going to put forth my best effort.' Now, what I have to say here is that it wasn't when the Bills scored to make it 35–10 that I remember, because you have to figure that at that point it was a give-me touchdown—and since that time I had been saying to Charlie, 'Oh, crap, now we have to go to our B and C material,' because the game was totally lopsided and we had an entire half to go. Because, as a broadcaster, there is nothing worse than what we were seeing, because there at that point of the game we couldn't make chicken salad out of you know what.

Anyway, like I said it wasn't that first Bills touchdown that made it 35–10, that I remember, that was the token one, but when Houston went three and out and the Bills scored again, that is the touchdown I remember the most, because it shouldn't have counted, because Don Beebe had been pushed out of bounds. He clearly stepped on the sidelines, we showed the replay again and again, and I said to our producer at the time—David Neal, who now is a super executive at NBC behind Dick Ebersol—I said to him, 'Save that picture of Beebe, because I think that it might be significant later on. Now, Rob, I'm not trying to tell you this all these years later, but I think any of them—Neal or Charlie, if he were still alive—would say it, too. Beebe clearly was pushed out of bounds by the cornerback and he stepped back in; Beebe caught the ball and all of a sudden the crowd was back in it and everybody starts looking at the clock and doing the math and saying, 'hey it may not be over,' but it was a touchdown that shouldn't have counted, because it wasn't close. Beebe was clearly out and once you step out, of course, you can't step back in.

Now, a couple of weeks later, I'm in New York doing sideline stuff and someone from the officials' office came to me and says, 'Look, I missed that one.' No, I was much younger then, I had better eyes, and the picture that I had Neal save clearly shows Beebe had stepped out. It reminded me of "The Music City" Miracle, where the Bills and everyone up there knows it—the Bills were on the other side of something similar. Now, was it a forward lateral? Sure it was, the tape shows it—if the guy throws it from the eighteen and it's caught on the twenty-one, do the math; it's a forward pass. But I sure wanted to tell the guy from the New York office off, but I was a young guy with the network, 34 or 35, and so I held my tongue. The plain truth is it was a forward lateral in Nashville; the plain truth is Tom Brady did fumble the ball and the plain truth is Don Beebe did step out of bounds.

Todd Christensen

* Todd Christensen was drafted by the Cowboys in the second round of the 1978 draft out of Brigham Young University. He was a member of the Los Angeles/Oakland Raiders from 1979–1988, twice led the league in receptions, was selected to five pro bowls, and was a member of the Super Bowl XV and XVII championship teams. Todd works for the Mountain West Sports Network.

CHAPTER SEVEN

*There were tremendous times in Buffalo during the Super Bowl years…
incredible players…great games. But the no-huddle offense is what I think helped
Jim Kelly become a hall of fame quarterback. Rob did you know that the no-huddle
offense began right there in Dunkirk, New York?*

*Rob, you have to check with others to see how they feel on this, but in my opinion, the
Buffalo Bills may not have gone to four consecutive Super Bowls, and Jim Kelly and all the
rest—Bruce Smith, Thurman Thomas, Marv Levy—they may not be in the hall of fame if
it were not for the no-huddle offense. It was the offense that propelled those teams and the
no-huddle was that offense.*

Somewhere over the course of one of our sit-downs Van and I began to
naturally discuss the Buffalo Bills of 2009, and the topic of the no-huddle style
of offense came up. I, as a fan, must be honest; I am thankful that the Bills
appear to be breathing some life into the offense by bringing back the no-
huddle or hurry-up style of offense. The won-loss record will say what needs
to be said though as to whether or not it helped.

*I don't want to say much about the 2009 Bills the season will tell the story, perhaps the
no-huddle might help, but when the no-huddle was here under Marv Levy Ted Marchibroda
was running it. Teddy was the Bills offensive coordinator during those great years, and he also
had spent time with the Philadelphia Eagles and was the former head coach of the Baltimore
Colts. He had quite a resume before he came to Buffalo. Ted was from Franklin Pennsylvania, and he played his college football at St. Bonaventure; it was a great school there in the*

Southern Tier, and it was while he was there in the late '40s and early '50s that he said he had first learned of the no-huddle offense from a guy named Mike Orbinati.

When Teddy was hired by Marv Levy to be his offensive coordinator he introduced to the Bills the no-huddle offense. It was a gradual introduction over the first couple of years. He and Jim Kelly collaborated on the no-huddle and used very simple terms to change the play and to get things moving. It wasn't complicated at all, but I believe because of that they made it to four Super Bowls.

First, it has to be said that Teddy Marchibroda was a helluva quarterback when he played for St. Bonaventure; and again, one of his teammates there was this guy Mike Orbinati. And it was Mike who had actually started the no-huddle style of offense at a small Catholic High School in Dunkirk—Cardinal Mindszenty High School—back in the '50s. Mike, when he was head coach there had set up a very simple system in which to use it. For example, he would yell 'red,' 'white,' or 'blue,' and if he yelled 'red' he'd want the ball snapped on one, 'white' on two, and 'blue' on three. A pass play might be numbered 25. So the quarterback without going into a huddle will yell red 25 and so there you had the play. That was how he did it early on, and it was there at St. Bonaventure, when he was a teammate of Teddy's, that he had shared the concept of it. That's how Teddy heard of it, how he was first introduced to it—to the no-huddle.

Ted knew how to play football and as a matter of fact, when St. Bonaventure dropped football, he transferred to the University of Detroit and became the nation's leader in yardage and would later play for both the Steelers and the old Chicago Cardinals. Teddy did, in some way, forget about Mike and the no-huddle, and some people will say that Cincinnati started the no-huddle under Paul Brown. But I say no, no sir; it began right down there at Cardinal Mindszenty High School in Dunkirk by Mike Orbinati. I also believe that without doubt it was Teddy Marchibroda and Jim Kelly that were responsible for getting the Bills to four Super Bowls and those teams had some all-time great players, some of the best ever to play, but without a doubt Teddy and Jim were the keys to the clicking on offense.

In later years he would bring it to Buffalo and incorporate it into the Bills offense, and he turned Kelly loose and Kelly loved it. Teddy just let Jim run it—Ted had no swelled ego either, he has never been a 'me guy,' an ego-driven guy, like a lot of coaches today. He gave credit where credit was due and he gave credit to Jim and to the receivers.

*Cardinal Mindszenty was the Primate of Hungary who, during the Hungarian uprising, sought refuge in the American Embassy. It was granted and he resided there for fifteen years. He had visited Dunkirk in the fifties and the school was named in his honor. The school closed in the seventies.

Ted Marchibroda

Coach, thank you for taking some time; it's a pleasure.

Sure, I am always happy to talk about the Bills and Van Miller; of course...he's a great guy. Van is one of the greatest personalities I ever came across and in all my years I never saw him unhappy. Van's a super guy who has lived a tremendous life and has done a great job for all of broadcasting. He has set the bar in many ways for those now in or who will be entering the field of sports broadcasting.

Yes, he has. He is becoming a quick role model for this 45-year-old when it comes to always being happy and enjoying every moment that life offers.

I'll agree with that. Van always had a smile on his face and would talk to anyone and everyone about anything.

Let's have just a little background so we can bring the readers up to date. I remember you from the '70s, as the head coach of the Baltimore Colts.

That's correct; I was head coach of the Baltimore Colts from 1975 though 1979. Bert Jones was our quarterback, Roger Carr was one of our key wide receivers; we had Raymond Chester at tight end and we had two great running backs with Roosevelt Leaks and Lydell Mitchell out of Penn State. In 1975—my first year there—we did win the division, the AFC East. We had a pretty strong defense, as well, with Stan White at right linebacker and Bruce Laird and Lyle Blackwood at safety.

You always did well against the Buffalo Bills in those days. I remember when I was a kid hating the Colts near as much as I did Miami. The Dolphins and the Colts were the tops of any young Bills' fan's hate list in those years.

Your coaching history is extensive; before you came to Buffalo you were offensive coordinator for the Washington Redskins, Chicago Bears, Detroit Lions, and Philadelphia Eagles. When did you come to Buffalo?

I came to the Buffalo Bills in 1987 as their quarterbacks' coach; and from 1989 to 1991, I was the offensive coordinator. I sat out a year, 1986, after having been with Philadelphia, prior to coming to the Bills.

Jim Kelly was already in place when you arrived, correct?

Yes he was. If I'm not mistaken, he had one year behind him already.

Marv Levy brought you in to work with Jim?

That's correct.

Van and I have spoken on several occasions about the no-huddle offense, and he has mentioned that the no-huddle—the hurry-up offense—actually began in the '50s in a high school there in Dunkirk. Could you elaborate on that just a little?

Well, Rob, I can't be totally sure that it wasn't used somewhere else before, so I can't give you a definitive history on that. But a kid I went to school with at St. Bonaventure named Mike Orbinati would later have the job as football coach at Cardinal Mindszenty in Dunkirk, and I remember him telling me along the way as our paths crossed that, in fact, the no-huddle had begun there at that Dunkirk Catholic school. So, as far as I'm concerned, that was it; I forgot all about it. And so, years later when Van and I got reacquainted and we talked about old friends and old stomping grounds, he reminded me of it and I said to Van, 'You know, I wished I had remembered that when the no-huddle was going on with the Bills, and I could have given Mike some credit,' but I had totally forgotten about it. So I guess until I see evidence saying something else, I will believe Mike and Van as to its origin.

Now, something else as far as the no-huddle—I remember this, too: I was driving to work one day with one of the assistant coaches—it was in the sixties, I think—and he said to me, 'You know, Ted, one of these days pro football will be played without using a huddle.' So I always remembered that. Also, later on—years later—something else I had forgotten about too was when I was with the Philadelphia Eagles. In 1985, I think, we had actually started the last game of the season with the no-huddle. We were out of it. Marion Campbell was the head coach and Ron Jaworski was our quarterback. So that's my story, as best as I remember, on the no huddle.

You had played quarterback yourself in college and had transferred out of St. Bonaventure to University of Detroit?

Yes. I did pretty well; I think I led the nation in total offense.

Then the Pittsburgh Steelers drafted you?

Correct.

Okay, jumping ahead—was the no-huddle in Buffalo used right away, as soon as you came?

No, we didn't really have it for a couple of years.

I noticed some of the win loss records: '88, 12-4; '89, 9-7; and '90, 13-3. As a casual observer of the game, it was clear once the proper personnel were in place in Buffalo, the no-huddle could be implemented. Also, in my opinion, Jim Kelly seemed perfect for the no-huddle. It seemed, again, only my opinion, that he would have struggled or not been nearly as successful coming out from under center.

Well, what I think really made the no-huddle work was that we had the players to run it, too. The guys we had knew their roles, and they perfected them, and we had the guy to pull the trigger in Jim Kelly. You look at who we had—James Lofton at one receiver, we had Don Beebe at the other receiver and we, by getting Lofton, Rob, we were able to move Andre Reed to the inside, and he was the perfect guy to play to the inside. He was a better inside receiver than he was to the outside, and after we got Lofton we could use Andre at his best. And then we had Thurman Thomas in the backfield—he could run, he could pass block, and, of course, we had a great offensive line.

In Buffalo it sort of grew. The no huddle started slowly and grew into a great machine. In other words, it was my system, the system I brought in, and when Marv hired me in '87, a large part of the system was already numbered. In other words, many of the pass and running plays were already numbered, and I'll give you an example.

We used to call plays such as…red right 27, 26 power,' sounds complicated to the non-football person, but it really is quite easy to understand. Well, we would run the plays so often that all we'd do after a while is just shorten them to red right 27, or 26 power. We were doing that when Tom Bresnahan became our assistant coach, one of my assistants, and when he came he said where he had come from that they used to number their formations, so now our numbering system was complete. The system already had numbers for snap counts, pass plays, and the running plays, so all we had to do was name the formation, and with the addition of Bresnahan, we were able to complete the package. When Tom numbered the formation, it shortened it even more; all we'd have to say now was 2-26, with 2 being the formation and 26 the play…understand?

Then all we had to do was to get the snap count, and if the call was 2-26 and Jim didn't say anything after that, the ball would be snapped on the very first sound; if Jim said 2-26 ducks, the ball would be snapped on 2—ducks being the code word for 2, because ducks go into the water 2 by 2. And if he said 2-26 crown, the ball would be snapped on 3, with crown being the code word for 3—you know, for the Triple Crown in horse racing. Then another thing, all our passes were already numbered, so all we had to say for passes were 2-91 crown—2 the formation, 91 the play, crown the snap count. It was very simple. Ultimately, it was naming the formation that Bresnahan brought that brought it all together.

And another thing, Rob, in the no-huddle, we didn't have a lot of plays. The guys knew what they were doing and Jim knew when to apply it. And what is and what was so important to know is—certainly what to do, but knowing when to do it is critical. Jim not only knew what to do he knew when to do it.

With Andre Reed to the inside, was his route to split the linebackers and safeties?

Well, Pete Metzelaars was the tight end, along with Keith McKellar, they were the K-Gun guys—K for Keith, I guess—but they were the tight ends and we had Andre on the inside. Beebe was outside of him and Lofton on the other side. Basically, four receivers, and if we wanted two tight ends, we took Beebe out. Don would go long, deep crossing, and Andre would go to the inside and pick his spot; they were good and they knew how to make the no-huddle work. But like Van said, it probably did begin there in Dunkirk. The no huddle was just developed over the years, and I think mastered, so to speak, in Buffalo.

When you came to the team in the eighties, what do remember about Van?

Well, what happened there too, Rob, is that in '53 or so I graduated St. Bonaventure and Mike Orbinati was head coach at Cardinal Mindszenty High School—their football team—and at that time he had invited me down to play in a charity basketball game. Van was also on the team in this tournament, and that was the first time I ever met Van; and you could tell at the time that he was just one great, outgoing guy. Van was a well-known, popular figure in the area at the time. He may have already been on the radio by then. But Van was gregarious to say the least. I think Steve Zajdel who also played with us in the tournament and was also from St. Bonaventure had told me at the time Van is a 'Bonnie guy,' which was the top compliment if you were from St. Bonaventure. He was a tremendous guy; he was as significant to broadcasting as anyone in the business may have ever been. When I came to the Bills we crossed paths more often, our roles didn't always allow us a great amount of time together but he was such a tremendous personality in Buffalo. The coaches knew it the players knew it. Van was a member of the media but he was part of the family

Knowing Van, though, is unique. He has been a tremendous voice for the Bills; he was an ambassador, in a way, for the Bills and the city, because wherever Bills fans were, might not always remember who the players were, because of the constant changes, but they knew Van was going to be the play-by-play guy. For so many people and for many generations he was the Buffalo Bills; and after all the years that had gone by, where we—he and I hadn't been in touch when we met each other again in the '80s, it was like it was the '50s all over again. We picked up right where we left off.

---

*Ted Marchibroda went on to be the first head coach of The Baltimore Ravens and just recently retired from the broadcast booth of the Indianapolis Colts. He's healthy and happy living in Virginia.

CHAPTER EIGHT

I did everything all by myself for years. I picked and played the records.
I scheduled the guests. I wrote and programmed the news. I never had a producer...
an intern...an assistant nothing until Paul Peck came walking through the doors.

I spent many years learning the trade. Not just how to broadcast...because you know I was broadcasting from the age of 10 though be it into a garden hose. At the same time I was without knowing it learning how to produce and even the skills needed to be an engineer. I had learned most everything that needed to be learned in radio so I didn't need an assistant because I knew how do everything and how to do it all in a timely manner. I had to be quick on my feet. It's the chicken and the egg again I did everything because I didn't have an assistant and once I knew how to do everything I didn't have a need for an assistant.

So with everything I had done at WFCB...with the variety of shows and all the football and basketball games I was very experienced by the time the other offers came along. I learned the techniques and the technical skills that were needed and I was well prepared. Later on offers came to me from other markets but I didn't want to leave Western New York. Certainly when I took the job with WBEN in 1955 I was ready and I believed I was prepared for that step.

WBEN had offered me a three-month contract in the summer of that year as a replacement announcer. I took the contract and the job and I stayed for 43...outstayed my welcome I think. WBEN was my big break, it was the one I was looking for and the one I certainly wanted so when the opportunity came to me I grabbed it. I stayed for those 3 months and then I began to call college games...football and basketball for the University of Buffalo and Niagara University. I stayed incredibly busy in those early years this is an excerpt from a morning paper. I don't know the date but it gives you an idea.

WBEN RADIO: begins its 21-game series of Niagara U basketball broadcasts at 8:20 this evening. Van Miller will be hoping on and off the gridiron between court contests.

Tonight the Purple Eagles go against University of Dayton. Van will broadcast the game direct from the campus field house in Dayton, O.

He'll log thousands of miles on these assignments.

For instance, after tonight's game he'll emplane for Tulsa for Friday's basketball encounter. Then he'll be football bound for the Bills' game in Oakland Sunday, return here Monday, handle a couple more basketball games then take off for Denver and the Bills' game on the 13th.

He'll also be in Boston Dec. 20th for the Bills-Patriots collision.

***

That story was just about one weekend or a week since it included two Bills road games. But I did everything and traveled everywhere. I was always in an airport it seemed heading to another airport. You know I have to wonder Rob if that opportunity hadn't come…the chance to work for WBEN so many other things may not have happened…but it did come. Things do happen for a reason and a lot of breaks came my way because I was in the right place at the right time but I also worked awful, hard and I paid my dues. So a combination of hard work and a little luck and things turned out the way they did.

But when WBEN came it gave me the big opportunity for with it came chances to do more on television. This was 1955 so TV was not very old at the time and their were some who didn't like the idea of television at all saying that it was a fad that'd soon disappear. As far as WBEN is concerned The Buffalo News originally owned the station and from what I learned the returning veterans from World War II built the transmitter and control room. The first studio there on the 18th floor of the Statler Hotel in downtown Buffalo. I might be wrong Rob so check this but WBEN may have been the only television station around including Rochester and parts of Pennsylvania.

Some of the stations' early shows were religious and one of the most popular show was one called "Meet the Millers," it was a show done by Bill and Mildred Miller who had a turkey farm in Colden. It was a small variety and cooking show and it lasted for a long time nearly 20 years…maybe longer. It was on the air for a long time.

At one time or another there was four of us doing sports at WBEN. There was Chuck Healy, Dick Riefenberg, Ralph Hubbell and myself. Dick Riefenberg had been a tremendous ball player at the University of Michigan and had led the nation in receiving his senior year and was drafted by the Detroit Lions but an injury early on ended his chance to play professionally. Chuck Healy would host one of the all time great bowling shows in Buffalo "Beat the Champ"…that was where whoever won a match one week would be challenged the following week and we had this one guy who was the champ for over twenty weeks.

I broadcast the first game of the Bills on September 11th 1960 against the New York Titans and with that one exception remained in the booth for 43 years. On top of Niagara University basketball, University of Buffalo, The Bisons' baseball, professional wrestling, golf tournaments, marathons and the afternoon show I did for so long "Norman Oklahoma" with Bill Peters who played Norman. I also hosted one of my favorite shows "It's Academic" it was a tournament of knowledge so to speak between groups of students from local schools.

I was always busy from sunup to sunset and loved every minute of it. But WBEN had so many great shows at the time, great kids shows one was "A Visit from Santa Clause", another kids show was "Uncle Jerry's Club"…this was a children's talent show…tap dancers, singers, piano players etc., there was the "Uncle Mike" show and "Fun to Learn" just a lot of good early shows that were popular for years. I took over the sports desk in 1965 and stayed for 33 years. WBEN became WIVB in 1977 when the Buffalo News sold the station to another publisher. WIVB stands simply for We're IV, the Roman numeral, we're for 4 Buffalo so WIVB stands for We're 4 Buffalo.

The Santa Clause Show and Uncle Jerry Show.

It was my time at WBEN that I think helped me land the job with the Bills in 1960 because I was becoming a known local voice. Early on Rob when we were at the Statler Hilton building we'd talk to anyone that would come through town and most folks who came through town wanted to stop in and talk to us. One of the most memorable for me was when Jane Mansfield stopped by for a chat…she was absolutely wonderful and incredibly gorgeous but sadly when she came by it was just a couple of weeks before her accident where she was killed.

I interviewed anyone and everyone that came through Buffalo. I talked to Bob Hope, Jane Mansfield, Mickey Mantel, the Dorsey band and Bob Feller the Hall of Fame pitcher of the Cleveland Indians. I even had a chance to interview John F. Kennedy when he was running for President at the time so it was early 1959 but I did it all by myself until Paul Peck came through the doors and I couldn't have been happier to meet a person in all my life than when he walked through the doors of the studio and I could have been happier when he did.

Van with Jane Mansfield just   Van with Mickey Mantle.
prior to her death.

Van with Hall of Famer Bob Feller.

As I gained experience at BEN I soon had many opportunities to leave Buffalo and go to other bigger markets in the '60s and '70s. Chicago, New York and all of the major networks had made offers too, NBC, CBS and ABC but leaving for New York City wasn't nearly as appealing as staying in an area I loved and that I called my home. Buffalo New York is our home and I wanted to stay here. I grew up in beautiful Chautauqua County. I swam and fished in Lake Erie, my grandfathers drowned in Lake Erie. The region, the city it was and will always be in my blood. I had to say too that my mother was there. I had to stay because I wanted to stay close to my mother.

Dunkirk as you may know Rob had the largest one-piece wooden flagpole in the world? It had stood in Memorial Park for many years the thing was enormous. It was so big that they brought it to Dunkirk up through the Panama Canal and how they ever got it up here only you know who knows...but anyhow...this region was and has always been our home...our roots were here. It was where I learned radio and again for decades I did everything by myself until Paul Peck came to the rescue and became my first producer. I couldn't have been happier to see a person in my life than when I first met Paul.

Paul Peck

Paul, Van had mentioned that at no time prior to you coming to WIVB did he ever have a producer of any kind so could I get just a little background…some things that the readers may not know about you? When did you come to the station?

It was in 1988 when I came to WIVB. I was fresh out of college. I had attended Syracuse University and graduated with a Degree in Communications. I had, like a lot of students who go for a degree in communications had aspirations of being an on-air broadcaster. I had as a student broadcast Syracuse football and basketball games I actually called the '87 National Championship game between Indiana and Syracuse where Keith Smart hit the final shot that won the game for Indiana 74-73. That was one of my first broadcasting highlights. I was working at the same student radio station where Bob Costas, Marv Albert, Dick Stockton and Mike Tirico had all worked at as students so it had a lot of history…a good pedigree of success so to speak and I knew I wanted to be on the air so getting some experience at a good student station with a good tree of success helped me. It was 1987-88 and I was working in New York City sort of as a production assistant and the job in Buffalo came up and besides being a full time job it was in a great sports market though it wasn't on air per se…so I said to myself fine, I'll do this for a little while…do what I have to do to learn what I needed to learn and have a full time job at the same time. I told myself that once Van saw what I was and what I wanted to do and certainly once he recognized the ability in me I would then have my chance to be an on air.

But I saw quickly that Van became my greatest fan and my greatest coach and he helped get me where I am now. Not only with the Bills Radio Network but also in doing play-by-play as well with the UB Bulls. Van was always an incredible, valuable resource on that I was lucky enough to make the transition from being a producer for Van to starting to get some on-air work here at Channel 4 and that of course eventually became full time. Now that's not necessarily how things work in this business. A lot of times you have to go to smaller markets like Binghamton or Elmira before you can come to a larger market such as Buffalo and do on-air. So Van was, at least I think such a driving force behind that for me. I don't know how much he went to the executives and said hey we have to get this kid on the air. I don't know if he did that or not but I think he might have said something like…this kid is pretty good and we need to start getting him on the air then I think that had something to do with it.

So you're at Syracuse University…working a part-time job in New York and you went the interview route at WIVB?

Well the News Director at the time was named Tim Morrison and he had just taken over as the News Director and he was a former Sports Producer himself and he sensed that Van as well as the department…the Sports Department, needed someone to run the show…well not run the show necessarily but someone to help behind the scenes. It was only Van, Brian Blessing and Glen Walker who were the on air guys. Tim felt that Van probably needed someone to help him out and I ended up getting the job by applying for it and by meeting those guys. I had not known that there had never been one…a producer prior to me…you know I was just out of college so this was a tremendous opportunity for me it was a big deal especially when I learned what it meant to work with Van and then it took on a whole different feeling…more than just a stepping stone that I initially thought it would be. I said this guy Van Miller is awesome and I'm going to learn a lot from him and I did.

Van seems that he is so unconventional it had to be difficult being a producer for him…at first anyhow?

Unconventional sure…he wasn't a black and white type of guy…he knew how to do it…the job and he knew how to do it right. But working with Van was incredible he enjoyed having me there and I think he welcomed my suggestions and if he liked them he'd take them and incorporate them into what he was doing and at the same time if he wanted to work something a different way then we'd do it his way. Van never felt…I don't think Van would ever say that he had to usurp some of the control over to me. I never felt that way. I was brought in to bring the shows together…to get them on the air and to make Van as comfortable as possible and to help him out and it worked well because I think we both had the same approach in that we wanted to work a bit unconventionally. I think the audience enjoyed it too.

You know what we did that may have been a little different was that if there was a great play from the night before from any game and any sport than we would have rather gotten that in than the standard Red Sox highlight. With that type of approach we started to do these weekly highlight shows and I'd save these highlights from the entire week and we'd play them on one of our broadcasts. I'd put five or six of these highlights in some kind of order I'd tell Van what I was thinking regarding the clips and he'd just run with it and he'd come up with great lines and just adlib stuff about something that would have everyone laughing and that's what worked out so great with it. I had to do was write something and he came up with all the rest.

Adlib is a great word when it comes to Van…he recorded a television commercial for us last year and he did it in one take unrehearsed it was amazing. The ability to think like that is Gods gift because as he has told me he was adlibbing Notre Dame games into a garden hose when he was just a little boy.

Sure it is, his ability to think on his feet is incredible. It really is unparalleled but that comes from doing play-by-play for all those years where you're on the air for three hours without a script. He had to think multiple moves ahead in order to anticipate anything and everything that might have occurred. He could do three hours easily so a three-minute sports segment was a breeze. Van never scripted any of his highlights out…all we did was…I'd take a sheet and I'd write out…3rd inning Don Mattingly RBI single…Yanks take 3-2 lead. The basic information is all he needed and he took it from there.

So Paul you came to the station when you were only 22 or so… you were 24 or 25 years old at the time of the Super Bowls?

That's right. I went to all four of them with Van and at the first one in Tampa he went absolutely nuts down there. We would do a show down there every night…you know right after the newscast we did a live from the Super Bowl show and we did an hour pre-game on Saturday…we went crazy down. It was the hardest I ever worked in my life but it was so much fun and Van at that first one was incredible he was so happy to be there. He had worked all his life and all he wanted was to see the Bills go to a Super Bowl and he was nuts. He was dancing around the lobby of the hotel with every woman he saw and he was hugging strangers and every Bills fan that was within shouting distance came up to Van they wanted to see him and be near him. He was in all his glory he was so excited to be there and I think it showed on the air. All he wanted I think was to be with the Bills when they went to a Super Bowl. He remembered what it was like of course during the AFL Championship years but this was different.

How do you…and I'm speaking from a fans perspective…how do you separate being a fan of the Bills and broadcasting or being part of the broadcast especially moments such as wide-right or the comeback game?

Sometimes it is hard I have to admit but we must be objective. But at the same time I think it's what made Van so popular and so legendary was that people could tell he was a fan. When they saw or met him they knew that he was a fan of the Buffalo Bills or Buffalo Braves. There is of course always a fine line that you have to walk in that regard...you have to understand that you're broadcasting to Bills fans but on the other hand you have to have some journalistic take on the game you're broadcasting by describing accurately what is taking place but deep down inside you want to see the home team do well because you know the people watching or listening want to see the Bills do well...but that is what Van was so good about, he was never over the top...nobody would ever call Van a homer. His enthusiasm and his excitement is what brought the fans in...he was a fan while not being a homer.

Two questions and I'll let you go. What is one experience you remember more than any others?

That's easy...there is one that I'll always remember...all my experiences with Van were incredible and I learned so much from him but there is one thing...one time that was classic Van. It was the third Super Bowl and we were in California and again we were doing this show every night after the newscast Monday through Friday, a live from the Super Bowl half hour show and we wanted to end the show each night by giving Van some opportunity to be funny. So it was during this period of time that most everyone was making fun of Jimmy Johnson's hair and that crazy hair he had...the hair that would never move so we decided that we'd end each show with the Jimmy Johnson hair update. We would ask one of the camera guys to take a close up of Jimmy Johnson's hair each day so we can give the viewers an update as to whether or not his hair had moved from the previous day...anyway that was the premise of how we were going to end each show each night during that week and every night Van would give a comical update on Jimmy Johnson's hair.

Now I will never forget we...Van and I were sitting in the stands on media day and the coaches for the Cowboys were at the podium and they'd take wave after wave of reporters down to ask their questions and I said to Van go down and ask Jimmy some questions...so Van goes down...and he asks him a couple of football questions at first and he said coach one last quick one and Vans says; Say Jimmy there is a reporter from Buffalo...some crackpot sportscaster that has been making fun of your hair every night...what do you think of that? Well I'm dying inside because of course it was Van who had been making fun of his hair all week and Jimmy Johnson in his real serious demeanor says...well I like to look good I think it's real important to maintain a clean, professional image at all time. Van kept such a straight face through it all and Jimmy took it all so seriously it was just classic Van. He could make fun of himself or anyone else...it was my favorite memory and we did after all did get the answer from the coach about his hair.

As best as you can Paul what has Van done for you...what have you learned from Van and what do you think he has done for the community?

Again Rob that's is an easy question. Van is the Buffalo Bills...this community...not only geographically speaking but also the Bills fan base is so tightly bonded to the Buffalo Bills and I would give Van some of that credit. He was excited when they won and he was disappointed when the lost. Back in the '60s when television wasn't what it is now Van was how people got to know about the new team in town, Van was their connection to the game. If the game wasn't on or they couldn't be there in person you would know that you could listen to the game and Van would tell you about it about everything that was going on the good, bad and ugly and more importantly just the way you were feeling it. He has a role in the Buffalo Bills history just like the players, Ralph Wilson and everyone in making the Bills so much a part of Buffalo and what he has done for me...you know...I do play-by-play now and I always think about what Van taught me about bringing the emotion through and paint the picture for the fan who is at home with their eyes closed...words...emotions mixed with fun and the ability to roll with the moment was what Van taught me. It's what he was the master of and of course personally Van is just a great guy and everyone loves him.

***

Rob, Paul and I worked well together. He is a good guy and is terrific at what he does and we made a good pair for the time we were together as I said earlier having him come through the doors of WIVB was a big relief.

So going back a little bit, staying in Buffalo was the best decision I ever made. After the station lost the Bills contract I could have gone other places but then the Braves came to town and the station did eventually get the Bills contract back. So that song or saying home is where the heart is...my heart is in Dunkirk...my heart is in this part of New York. I know we've talked about this but Dunkirk is a garden spot. I did fun, innocent things there with my friends. We didn't have the peer pressure that the young people of today have. I can remember back to my Bedford Products days where I worked and where I had the terrible accident...I worked alongside German prisoners of war during the Second World War. They never caused any problems they always were looking for cigarettes though. I didn't smoke but that didn't stop some of them from asking me the same question every day.

I had the opportunities to move up to those bigger cities...but my mother didn't want to go and I wasn't going to leave her she raised me without any help. My father abandoned me as a babe-in-arms and he abandoned her. I was meant to stay in right where I was.

There was a brief time in the '70s...well not so brief it was seven years when you weren't the voice of the Bills.

That's right...I wasn't real happy about it either. I had been broadcasting Bills games since their inception in 1960 but in 1972 WKBW purchased the broadcast rights to the games and hired Al Meltzer to take my place...he was from Philadelphia...but I sure stayed busy during those years. I became the voice of the Buffalo Braves of the NBA and I called all the Braves games right up until they left for San Diego in 1978 and became the Clippers.

You know I was in Junior high when the Braves were here; I have to say I wasn't the biggest of NBA fans...except Dr. "J" at the time but I do remember the Braves had some very good players.

Oh my yes...they had Gar Heard, Randy Smith...who passed away not long ago...they had Bob Kauffman...they had Elmore Smith he was over 7 foot, they had Ernie DiGregorio and of course they had one of the all time greats in Bob McAdoo. He was rookie of the year the year he came to the Braves. Jack Ramsay was by far their best coach. They were only here eight years or so and had about as many coaches but Jack Ramsay was the best and he did go on to win the NBA championship with Portland after he left Buffalo.

The Bills returned to WBEN in 1979 and everyone came back with to the booth with you...your spotters and stats guys correct?

Oh yea...they all came back and of course if I had gone to New York or another one of the bigger markets who had courted me during the interim I'd never have come back...and I would have missed everything.

The '80s, especially the early years were some pretty bad years for the Buffalo Bills…speaking from the point of view of someone who sat at home watching and complaining.

There were some bad years but when the team is doing well, the fans love the players, they loved Ralph and they loved me…but when the team is losing…no body wants to listen to a bad, one way…lopsided game…they can go do something else that is just as lousy or boring and perhaps not get frustrated along the way.

"The Super Bowl of eating."

This is a great story Rob. It was the early '60s and the Bills had a home game coming up on Sunday. It was over about 2:00 p.m. or so and a couple of them piled into this station wagon. There were three of the behemoths Jim Dunaway, Ron McDole and Paul Mcguire along with their wives and they headed to Rusch's Restaurant in Dunkirk. Now Rusch's Restaurant had a Friday Night Special. It was all you can eat Lobster Dainties for $3.95. You would get four or five Lobster Dainties plus fries with your original order. Now they get to the restaurant around 4:00 p.m. and even in Dunkirk no one eats at that time so the restaurant was empty. The waitress recognized the Bills players and she got excited. McDole and Dunaway had a bet on who could eat the most Lobster Dainties; it was a $20.00 bet. They ate their first plate and a second. The waitress made trip after trip to the kitchen for plate after plate of these Lobster Dainties and the cook finally wanted to know how people were out there. The waitress said that there was only one table but that it was a couple of Buffalo Bills having an eating contest.

Well I tell you it was the Super Bowl of who could eat the most and as Dunaway told me we they had got to 70 when the butter had started to get to him and he and McDole agreed to quit at 77 a piece. Jim wanted to save room for desert but by this time the owner Danny Rusch was there and he goes up to the table and says that look we love to have you Bills players here but don't ever come back on a night when we have an all you can eat special. Danny had to place a last minute reorder of Lobster Dainties for the dinner crowd yet to come in. Well they finished eating and headed back and by the time they got to Silver Creek about 10 miles away McDole reached into his pocket pulls out a handkerchief and pulls out one more Lobster Dainty and swallows it. He looks at Jim and said that's 78, I win, you owe me $20.00.

CHAPTER NINE

*The higher up lost the contract or let the contract rights go to broadcast
the Bills games—a tremendous plus for me, though, was I had the chance to call
the games for the Buffalo Braves.*

Van, I spoke with Elmore Smith, the former Buffalo Braves center, and he said that you were, without a doubt, the kindest, fairest, most-honest member of the media he ever dealt with during his playing career.

That's kind of Elmore to say; he was a big guy out of Kentucky State. Over seven feet, he was the first center taken in the 1971 draft, and I'm pretty sure he was the second or third overall pick that year.

You know, Rob, I have said this before, I'm sure, but in broadcasting, you run into a lot of characters, especially doing play-by-play for as long as I did without missing a game. Fifty-five years. But I have to say that the Buffalo Braves, you had to go some to beat the type of people you met during the days of the Buffalo Braves. I was the team's only play-by-play guy and I did every game in the team's eight-year existence here in Buffalo. It is too bad that they aren't here now, but I don't know if the region could support three major sports; but for a couple of years, Buffalo did just that.

Braves promotional advertisement, courtesy Steve of Cichon.

Ralph Wilson made Buffalo a major league city and in 1971 Cleveland, Portland, and Buffalo were all granted NBA franchises and Eddie Donovan was the Braves first general manager and the first coach was Dolph Schayes. He had come from Philadelphia where he had been coach of the year at one time. They had some difficult years early on, winning only a few games their first couple of years—just twenty their first year—but they had some great moments, too, like the playoff match ups against the Boston Celtics. The excitement was tremendous in the auditorium during those playoff games; it was some of the best I ever experienced. The aud was standing room only every night. One of the lows I thought, besides the bad years on the court was when the Braves did not draft the All-American Calvin Murphy—crying out loud, he was right here at Niagara University. He was pound for pound one of the best there ever was to play. The Braves chose John Hummer out of Princeton, who did have a couple of good years, but was not a Calvin Murphy.

WBEN advertisement highlighting Calvin Murphy and Van, courtesy of Steve Cichon.

There were many, many fun times there at the aud with the Braves and the fans, of course; you know they were right there on top of the players and on me and they were loud. There was another time, in order for me to interview Wilt Chamberlain; I had to stand on one of the team's equipment trunks. You know he was over seven feet and weighed over 250 pounds. But what a lot of people may not know is that before he ever got into professional basketball, he had played for the Harlem Globetrotters. There was the night, too, when Phil Ranallo, the sports columnists for the old Buffalo Courier-Express, wasn't only thrown out of the game, but he was thrown out of the auditorium for chastising the referee after each and every one of his calls. The ref had had enough and stopped the game entirely in order to throw Phil out the door; anyway, it was very different back then.

I would call the games pretty much on my own without any help; sometimes, most times, I would have a scorer, but I was it. I would do the six o'clock news at WBEN TV and then rush over to the game, do the game, some post-game interviews, and then fly back to the studio for the eleven o'clock news. I had no producer, no assistant, no intern. It was hectic, but it was fun.

Wilt Chamberlain as a Harlem Globetrotter.

I can't express it enough; I absolutely loved every minute of my experience with the Braves. I would sit right close to the end of the Braves' bench, and whether you or anyone else knows it or not, Rob, I was one of Dr. Jack Ramsay's assistant coaches. For instance, when Dr. Jack had pulled Randy Smith or Ernie D. because they had picked up a third foul, and if I thought they had sat out long enough and they needed to be back on the court, I would just say, loud enough for Dr. Jack to hear me, 'Randy Smith has been sitting out; I can't help but wonder when he'll get back onto the court.' Dr. Jack would hear my always-above average broadcast moment and instantly send Randy back in. We were a great team.

The Braves' leaving town for San Diego was a dark day, to be sure. Randy Smith died way too young. And for me, there is or was no better coach than Dr. Jack Ramsay, as I had said, I'm sure. He did go on to win that NBA Championship with the Portland Trailblazers—he is, in my opinion, the best coach I ever had the privilege to know. Jack Ramsay was one of the best coaches in history, and when the Buffalo Braves got Bob McAdoo, he would be one of the best ever to play the game. With him, the Braves became a playoff team, and I think he can still out-shoot any of the young guys now.

Bob McAdoo

You have to answer a question that has been with me since I was a little kid growing up in Western New York. I remember hearing a song that was making its way across the airwaves called The Bob McAdoo song. It went, "McAdoo... McAdoo...McAdoo..."

Yea, Randy Smith did that. He wrote it and he and a couple of other guys sang it; I think it came out during my second year.

Who's going to dribble that ball down the court?
...McAdoo, McAdoo, McAdoo.
Who's going to make that lay-up and score?
...McAdoo, McAdoo, McAdoo.
Who's going to steal that ball on you?
...McAdoo, McAdoo, McAdoo.
Who's going to snatch that rebound too?
...McAdoo, McAdoo, McAdoo.

Big Mac...Big Mac...McAdoo, McAdoo, McAdoo.

What's our team got, you aint got?
...McAdoo, McAdoo, McAdoo.
Who's the guy that's going to block that shot?
...McAdoo, McAdoo, McAdoo.
Who's the best scorer in the whole league?
...McAdoo, McAdoo, McAdoo.
Who's the best center you ever did see?
...McAdoo, McAdoo, McAdoo.

That's it! I think about it every now and then. I think about Randy Smith all the time of course. He died a young man.

Van with Fred Hilton and Randy Smith, courtesy of Steve Cichon.

You and he are always named as two of the fans favorites when it comes to Buffalo Braves. Just a little background if we can. You were drafted in 1972 by the Buffalo Braves, second overall, ahead of Paul Westphal and Dr. J?

Yes, I was. Remember that "J" went to the ABA; he went over and played for the New York Nets of the American Basketball Association. There was still the ABA at the time and both leagues were drafting guys, it was good for the players because we could choose to go to the highest bidder. I had been drafted by the ABA, as well, and was the second overall pick in the NBA.

What made you choose the NBA over the ABA?

For me, it was an easy choice, because it was the NBA. It was the dream of every little kid to grow up and play in the NBA. The contract was better, too, but I felt the league, it was historic and was more stable. I could make my mark there in the NBA, rather than in a new league, which may not be around in a couple of years.

You came out of North Carolina?

Yes, I did. Well, I transferred from Vincennes Junior College in Indiana to North Carolina, and then I was drafted from there. Being drafted by Buffalo, you know we had all seen the reports of all the snow. We had played in the cold and some snow, but nothing like Buffalo, of course, so that would be a quick change for me.

The first year, 1972 was an ugly one.

Yes, it was an ugly one; we ended the season 21-61. When I get to Buffalo, Dr. Jack— Jack Ramsay—was the coach, he had drafted me and, to be honest, I thought I was good enough to start right away. He, Dr. Jack and I didn't get along, initially, because of that. Dr. Jack was an old-time coach. He was of the old school and he wanted rookies to be brought along slowly before they got their start. But when Bob Kauffman went out with an injury, I went in and never sat back down on the bench again after that.

When you came to the Braves you were a power forward. Could explain what the difference between a power forward and regular forward, for lack of a better word?

Sure, I was a power forward slash center. The primary difference is that a power forward is anywhere from six-eight to six-eleven and works underneath the basket. They are the muscle guys on the inside, whereas a small forward works from the outside—essentially a bigger guard, in most cases, they are the guys who can set a good pick. I was, I guess, the one who changed that because I was a power forward who could shoot from the perimeter, as well.

I have to say this the auditorium...the aud, playing there was tremendous. When I shot and got hot from the outside or got on a run the fans seemed like they were everywhere. It was a close environment; the fans absolutely loved the Braves, especially when we would take the Washington Bullets and Boston Celtics to a seven-game series. The environment there was super. Buffalo loved their basketball, and when the team left, there for were a lot of upset folks. I played in other places—New York and Los Angeles—but Buffalo is the city where I started my career. I began my family there. I played twenty years in professional ball, and have been in coaching over fifteen years, but it began there in Buffalo.

You were rookie of the year and won multiple scoring titles and league MVPs while you were here.

That's right; I learned from a great coach in Dr. Jack. He is one of the best of all time. We didn't get along at first, but I learned what I needed to and learned so much about how to be an NBA player from my introduction into the league there in Buffalo.

You mentioned that you began your family here in Buffalo. Van had told me about one night when "Little Mac" ran onto the court.

That's right. One time in a game there at the aud, my wife was walking in at one end of the court and the game had just started, or was a few minutes old. My little boy sees me and began to squirm. He was just a couple of years old. I had taken the inbound pass and my son sees me, gets away from my wife, and runs onto the court, chasing me down. The game had to be stopped so I could take him back to my wife. He's a tennis pro now in New York.

You know Rob I hadn't thought about Van for some time, until you called, but every now and then a memory of Van would pop up. I would recall a game or a joke he may have told. He was such a tremendous broadcasting force up there. I don't think he ever had an enemy though. He was fair with everyone, he never went after any of the players and we really respected that. I sure don't remember players saying anything negative about him. Van was professional in every meaning of the word when it came to his job but I think he liked to have fun too.

Van, he was the voice of Buffalo. Pretty simple: he did every one of our games, but before the Braves started to play, he had done the Bills and the local news. He was the voice that everyone came to know. I remember seeing him do the news, do play-by-play for us, and later do the news on the same night. He was always there; he never missed a game and treated me honestly and fairly during all my years there and that may have been the only place to treat me that way.

Van did that. He would do the six o'clock newscast, run down to the auditorium, do the game, do his post-game interviews, and make it back to the station to do his eleven o'clock newscast.

Yea, Van was the voice of Buffalo, not just the Braves or the Bills, but he was the voice of Buffalo. He loved to do our games. We'd sit on the bench, which was close to where he would broadcast from, and we'd watch him get excited about a call or a bad call and we'd see how he'd react when one of us made a big play on the court. It was so easy to tell that he was a fan of basketball; the team and everyone loved him and respected him.

Let me tell you this one story about Van—maybe it was Van, I don't know, but it was how it was told to me. This is the one story that comes to me as clear as day. It was after I had been traded to the New York Knicks in December of seventy-six for a player and cash; it was towards the end of the season and I was getting ready to come back to Buffalo for the first time since being traded. A friend of mine in Buffalo calls me up and says, 'Mac, I can't believe you said what you said—it's in the papers and even Van Miller is talking about it. It's all over town.

Well, I didn't know what he was talking about, so I asked him, 'What did I say, supposedly?' Well, my friend says that I had declared that if the Knicks go into Buffalo and lose to the Braves that I would walk back to New York City. I couldn't believe it. I had a lot of friends in Buffalo. I would have never said something like that. I think the fans still liked me, but when I was introduced and came running out onto the court that night at the aud, I was booed off the planet. I couldn't believe it. Then I took my first shot of the game and it was an air ball and 15,000 people were now laughing at me. I couldn't believe it. I was mad and now my hair was standing on end by then. So I went nuts, scored 38 points, and we won the game. I can't prove he did it, but I think Van might have at least encouraged the story of my walking back to New York at least a little—it didn't matter, regardless. Van is a tremendous person. He was always fun and fair and he loved his teams; he loved his job. My time there was terrific; like I said, it was where it all began for me, and Van Miller treated me better than any other members of the media of the day. He will always be a credit to his craft and certainly someone any future broadcaster should seek to emulate.

---

*Bob McAdoo was NBA Rookie of The Year in 1973. In 1974 and 1975, he was the league's Most Valuable Player. He led the NBA in scoring for three consecutive years and would play for the New York Knicks, The Boston Celtics, and the Los Angeles Lakers, with whom he won championships in 1982 and 1985. In 2000, he was elected to the Pro Basketball Hall of Fame. He has been an assistant coach for the Miami Heat for the last fifteen years.

CHAPTER TEN

Precious Heavenly Father, hundreds of miracles happen every day. Thank you for them today. Help me to recognize them and to allow them to happen. What a day it is going to be!
-God's Minute-

The comeback game was my greatest broadcast even considering all the Super Bowls and the two AFL Championship games it was an incredible day for everyone in the booth that day…now speaking of booth have I told you this story I like to call it…

"I'll get you the best…I swear it."

This is a true story Rob and it's about a spotter I had one time. A spotter is a person, a helper of mine who sat in front of me, there was one on my left and another on my right…mine were Dr. Ed Gicevich, Dr. Bob Werner and Dick Dobmeier and one would be responsible for the home team and the other the visiting team. The spotter would tell me what player made a play, a tackle or a catch or a key block and they'd also have a pieces of information about the player such as the school they attended…hobbies etc. The offense would be on one side of the spotting board and the defense on the other side of the board. Now this story is about the time I had a one-eyed spotter.

Now I never had any trouble with spotters at home, in Buffalo, I had my guys and I knew the Bills players well enough but it was on the road where I had trouble and if I couldn't get a local guy I'd have to hire one. This time, this one particular day we were in Cincinnati playing the Bengals and I was going to need a spotter to help me call the Cincinnati side of the ball. I would do the Bills and I would have to get a local guy to handle Cincinnati. So I call their P.R. guy Al Hyme and I told him I needed a spotter. I'll pay him decent money and he can have all the food he can eat in the press box. Al said no problem Van I'll get you the best…I swear it don't you worry.

So we get to Cincinnati and I'm in the booth and in walks this guy and he was wearing rose colored glasses…you know, very dark sunglasses and it's about forty-five minutes before the game. This guy walks in and says I'm your spotter and you should know that I have never done this before…ever. I mumbled words that were better off mumbled and said thank you Al "I'll get you the best" Hyme.

The game is only minutes away and this guy had never done spotting before at any level much less the pros so I had to give him a quick lesson on what he needed to do. The game was just about to start and he wouldn't take his glasses off. So because we only had a few minutes to go before kickoff I went over the spotting board with him and gave him some basic hand signals so he could let me know who deflected the ball, made a big hit etc. He said no problem and so the game starts and he's got these damn sunglasses…these rose colored glasses on…he wouldn't take them off for the kickoff or even for the first couple of series. He's supposed to be spotting for Cincinnati and he's giving me nothing…I mean absolutely nothing. Another series goes by and I'm getting mad and we went for a commercial break and I said to him look I'm paying you and I want you to help me a little bit here…let's work together on this so give me a little something at least. I know where the ball is on the field and who has it but you can help with a tackle at the very least.

He said to me, I have to tell you this too. I'm having some trouble…trouble I asked…he said yes I am seeing everything double. Double…what do you mean you're seeing everything double? I'm just seeing everything double. I told him what you do… just take the damn number and divide by two but for Gods sake try to give me a little help. Well then he rips off his dark glasses and says I guess I should have told you this before but I just had eye surgery on my left eye and I can't see a thing. I didn't know what to say. So Al "I'll get you the best" Hyme gave me a one-eyed spotter with no experience in Cincinnati.

There is another one…another story about a local guy. I won't use his name naturally and we were on the road in Miami. This guy had infiltrated a party being held by the owner of the Miami Dolphins Joe Robbie. It was first thing in the morning on game day…like 9-10:00 and we were at the Orange Bowl in Miami and Robbie was having this party right up close to where the press sat and the coaches boxes were. Anyway this guy, my spotter, infiltrated this party and mingled for a couple of hours with all the hoi polloi and this party had started very early in the day…well before the kickoff…well he mingled alright…he mingled and mingled and mingled.

He was my spotter and it was an hour or less before kickoff and I was getting ready for the game and he walked into the booth with just a few minutes to go. I didn't know it at the time but he was drunker than a skunk when he left the Joe Robbie party and took his seat in the booth. Now I thought he looked kind of funny when he walked in but I was too involved in what I was doing to pay much attention but I asked if he was sick. He mumbled yea, yea I'm fine. The game starts and the Bills receive the kickoff and they get called for a cut block during the return and this guy staggers up to his feet and shouts down to the field a mouthful of four letter adjectives many of which were new to me. I couldn't believe this guy and he went on and on using every word there was in the book. I had to wait until a commercial break and then I had to go and get a security guard or a cop to come get this guy out of the booth so I went and did without that day. So anyway sometimes on the road we had trouble getting spotters and these two stick out gloriously among all those I had...but my guys they were the best...Ed Gicewicz, Dick Dobmeier, Bob Werner, Mike Mullane, and Art Plant.

***

From the first time we met Van Miller he called us buddy and he has referred to Kendra as my bride and my better half, both of which are true.

Every subsequent phone call and every visit Van called me buddy. His former broadcast partner Greg Brown said that I would quickly discover, if I hadn't already that he calls everyone buddy. That is true whether you are a first time visitor or longtime acquaintance you our Van's buddy. So after some thought I concluded that this chapter should be dedicated to Van's buddies...the folks who have known him for many decades and who have worked with him from the first whistle in 1960 to the final one in 2003.

Dr. Ed Gicewicz

Dr., Van, a couple of years ago had begun talking to my wife about the game we were watching at the time, the Jets and the Bills it was Trent Edwards first start as quarterback. And before I had noticed she had become a new victim for Van to unveil his humor. I couldn't help but over hear when he asked Kendra what happened to her other earring.

Oh sure Van has used that particular line for as long as I've know him…and without fail the woman will always reach for her ear. It's his way of breaking the ice. Van does do just what you've said Rob he draws anyone and everyone in with his humor. Van is an incredible individual, professional and on a personal level and I'm sure you have this but it is my understanding that Van had no experience in big time broadcasting except that he had done many high school and college games before he was hired by the Buffalo Bills.

Yea there was that and The Farmers Exchange and of course professional wrestling while he was at WFCB.

It was highly unusual to hire a guy like that…like Van as an announcer for a professional football team. If I remember at the time he auditioned for the job and after they had screened everyone else they…the Bills picked Van even though he had no experience at that high a level of competition. Not to say that he didn't deserve it but from what I remember he went head to head against some guys who had the quote unquote the national, big-stage experience.

Now we, my wife and I, have known Van and Gloria going back many…many years we became social friends and Gloria is the God mother of my first son so we were friends before I ever started working for him. I first got involved with Van because I was a high school and collegiate football referee and in the early days there were some questions about the interpreting of the rules. One weekend Van asked me to come with him to a game or two to help interpret the official's calls or to better explain a particular ruling on the field. When the flag went up I would help him out. So it's pretty simple one time Van just asked me to come along and I ended up working with him for decades…he roped me in so to speak.

I did some basic things at first and after that the person that handled the Bills stats left…he may have been Vans cousin Jimmy Georgeson I believe I took his place.

This had to be real early because Van and I were together nearly forty years so it was 1962 or '63 and from that point on I'd sit to the right of him and the other spotter Dick Dobmeier sat to the left of him and whenever a key play happened our job was to identify the player. On the spotting board was the players basic stats…height, weight, his college…what year he graduated and any other interesting comments about the player that Van might be able to make. We had the offense on one side of the board and the defense on the other side of the board so when the ball possession changed we just flipped the board over.…so that's how I got started with him.

Dick Dobmeier...the guy on Van's left always was the spotter for the visiting team or opposition if we were on the road. The opposition spotter was on Van's left and I did the home team and I was on his right.

I'm just curious but were there any two-way players still with the Bills when you spotted in the early years? Were there players on both sides of the board?

No, I don't believe so...well the only one that comes to mind without thinking to hard is "Cookie" Gilchrist...he was a helluva' linebacker and...do you know his history?

No sir just some of the basics.

He was in my opinion the toughest, hardest hitting, hardest knocking back...fullback in those early years. "Cookie" was unstoppable with just that sheer brute strength of his he could get through any hole and sometimes when the Bills were forced into making a goal line stand "Cookie" would go in as a linebacker and he was a very, very tough customer when he played linebacker too. But as far as I know there was no one else with the Bills that went both ways. In early days of college when I played at The University of Buffalo...when I played we went both ways and even in the early days of the pros the only guy that I can think "Cookie" was it.

You were with Van during those AFL Championship days and I can't think of the AFL days without remembering Jack Kemp.

Van and Jack Kemp circa 1965.

Jack Kemp and I got to be very close. I traveled with Van and the team early on but later I became the team doctor for the University of Buffalo and I had to give up traveling to road games. In college you'd work out on Friday for a Saturday game...play on Saturday and if you were away you'd return on a Saturday night and in the pros they left on a Saturday and so I couldn't do that because of my medical obligations to the University. Van would get someone else to do the boards for him on the road...but anyway we were talking about Jack Kemp.

When I traveled with the Bills the guys would get on the plane and you know there were the rowdy ones and there were other guys playing cards and those that'd just sleep and I would always sit next to Jack on the plane. He be totally absorbed in a book he'd always be reading...not a novel but some obscure book on history of economic theory or something similar. He was brilliant, incredibly mentally gifted. If I remember right he was major in history at Occidental...he loved and appreciated history and we became good friends and remained friends right up to his untimely death this year. When he made his run for Congress I was very active in his campaign and I'd set up places and dates and I would be the one that would introduce him to various groups. Jack ended up winning the seat for Congress and though I never had a tremendous zeal for politics he did get me involved in it to the degree that I did.

The work I did for him in '96 was so basic. I was the balloon and chair guy and he traveled with his son Jeff and Ernie Ladd. Ernie was the former ball player and teammate of Jacks with San Diego and had also been a professional wrestler. Now Ernie was one big guy an easy four-hundred pounds and he'd regularly stand behind Jack Kemp on stage and during one such occasion…Ernie who had tremendous difficulty standing by this time asked if he could lean on me for some support…he leaned on my shoulder for well over an hour…an adventure in pain I assure you.

I remember Ernie who was quite a professional wrestler.

Off hand do you recall any Van moments?

Oh there are always Van moments but there was this one time…there were many but there is always one that comes back to me. We were on a West Coast swing and were in San Diego first and after that we'd head up to Oakland or over Denver I can't recall the exact order. So we played the San Diego Chargers and I had this pal of mine who lived in Las Vegas and he picked us up after the game and we drove over to Las Vegas. We had a week to kill before the next game so we'd figure we'd do it there. I remember we at the Sahara and I was at the gaming tables…craps or roulette one of them and I was doing real well. I was ahead quite a bit and Van walks up to the table. I saw his approach out of the corner of my eye. Van takes a seat at the table and he started to bet against me and in virtually no time he took all my money I had won and plenty more. Has Van mentioned that yet…that he took all my money on a road trip?

No this one he hasn't told me, he may have overlooked it.

Well he hurt me…in jest of course. I was ahead quite a bit before he sat down and by the time the next couple of hours had passed us by I was out of chips and largely to his advantage. Let me tell you this too…this is a small little one, but again we were in Oakland and they had a very primitive stadium at the time. It was nothing but bleachers and the press box was just above the highest row of seats and a guy named Valley owned the Raiders. I can't remember his first name...Wayne perhaps and he and his wife sat right in front of us...I mean I could reach out and touch the lady. She was wearing this fine coat as you might imagine an owners wife might wear when in public and we were doing our broadcast and I had a Coke bottle in front of me and as I mentioned we had offense on one side and defense on the other side of the spotting board and as I was flipping the board in order to get to the pertinent side I knocked the Coke bottle over on to the owners wife...her fluffy quaff...I couldn't have ever been more apologetic then I was that day but to my relief they both handled it in stride.

The owner *was* Wayne Valley...he...from my recollection was responsible for hiring Al Davis away from the Chargers. In what I discovered during my research, is that Al Davis took to doing things the way he saw fit and not necessarily the way the owner wanted things done. For instance when Valley was overseas attending the 1972 Olympics in Munich Davis drafted a new memorandum, which virtually gave him complete control over the Raiders.

Al hasn't changed much to the detriment of the Raiders I believe.

Did you work for WBEN, the Bills or just Van?

I went with Van...when BEN lost the contract we went our own way and when BEN got the Bills contract back they brought the whole team back as well.

If you had to pick your time top three games what would they be?

The comeback against Houston...the Oilers that is high on my list and is probably high on the list for anyone that had a part in the game or its broadcast I'd say...that was a spectacular experience. That hit on Lincoln...Keith Lincoln the Chargers All-Pro running back...when Mike Stratton broke his ribs and knocked him out of the title game that was the difference. The Bills played a helluva' game there that day in '64 and as I remember they were not the favorite the Chargers who were loaded...it was a Championship game...'64 out there at War Memorial Stadium. Then there was a game in which the Bills would eventfully win our part of the league...we were in Boston and the field was covered with snow and the officials had the field marked in red and it was a snowy, wet, cold nasty day. We were at Fenway because that's where the Patriots played then and there were no doors and no windows to the press box and we were frozen and a guy named Shonta...I think that was it...regardless, "Cookie" nailed him and the Patriots fumbled which as I recall was the difference in the game and that allowed them to go to the Championship Game. Fenway was an interesting place to broadcast a game from and I don't think I had ever been as cold as I was that day.

Wide right of course is a game I will never forget. I can't believe this city has been at the short end of stick because of a wide right kick and because of an illegal goal against the Sabres. It was that game where it went into over time after over time after over time...I think there were five altogether and it ended about 2 a.m. in the morning. The Super Bowl games of course when Thurman Thomas couldn't find his helmet, the biggest game you'd ever play and he couldn't find his helmet...everyone was screaming up in the press box.

That might be what Bruce Smith was referring to at this years Hall of Fame induction. He paused during his speech he paused, looked at Thurman and admitted that he was the one that hid his helmet.

Now that you mention it that does sound familiar but wow...the biggest day and one of your great players has a trick played on him. For me Van is a tremendous role model for those wanting a career in radio. He is one of my best friends and sharing all that we have; well it was just some remarkable times.

Van in the booth his hand is resting between the spotting boards.

Dick "Dobby" Dobmeier

I know you have been battling some health issues so thanks much for taking time and chatting here for a little while.

Sure it's great to be home though after spending a good chunk of time in the hospital and besides I have to talk about Van. Van is a remarkable person. Rob probably you have heard that a thousand times by now but it can't be over emphasized when it comes to him...he really is a success story, coming from nothing and through hard work and perseverance he got where he did.

I have known Van since 1960, perhaps a little earlier. We got to know each other because our daughters went to the same grammar school together and he and Gloria just lived a block away. Van's daughter and my daughter were the best of friends and Van would take them skiing on Saturday up to Kissing Bridge and as a matter of fact Jack Kemp taught my oldest daughter how to ski.

I have asked this of others but how well did you know Jack?

I knew him quite well. Now I don't know how you'll write this Rob but one time we were down in Miami at the Orange Bowl and Jack had talked to someone before the game and was told that he could be the color commentator. I was the spotter and I spotted both teams that day...at that time they, Bills radio, experimented with having a visiting color man and this one day Jack was in Miami and he said he'd do it. Now he comes to the booth like three minutes before kick-off and asks us...what do I do? The looks on our faces said tons but I told him where to sit and that Van will do what he does and we would give him a hand signal or some sign as to what to say and when to say it. Well at the kick-off or the first series and Jack leans down to me and says I can't see the damn field...so we had to go and get a small TV and set in front of him so he could see the field better. That's how he worked that day.

How did Van get you involved with the broadcasts?

We were at 'The Rockpile' and Van had a lot of friends and he'd invite a bunch of us to the games and we'd hang out around the box. Van decided that he needed to make each one of us useful to him so in one way or another each of us would help compliment his broadcasts. At first each of us would do something different one guy would do first downs…the other one would keep track of receptions and another passing. We carried little spiral notebooks with us and kept track of the yardage and we'd hold it up and when Van wanted the information he'd turn around and take a look. It was easy and I think complimented Vans work quite well.

As the years went by Ed Gicewicz was the spotter on Van's right so you'd be the board on his left side?

Yes the initial group of fifteen or so got smaller and smaller and it developed into Dr. Bob Werner, Dr. Ed Gicewicz and myself. I was on Van's left and I did both games for many years…home and away because we didn't people going out and spotting for us on the road so I did travel with the Bills.

As a spotter my job was to keep track of the players…who's going in who's out…who made the catch, tackle etc. We always wanted to have some information on the player…their schools…personal records or just some interesting facts that Van might be able to use in the course of the game.

Did you have any experience before Van asked you?

No just association with the sport and all sports. I went to Niagara University so I had a fans knowledge of the game and it helped me to transition to the spotting board quite easily.

Did you assist Van during the Buffalo Braves time in Buffalo?

Yes most of the seven years. The first couple of years for the Braves were lean and mean and we usually broadcast on Tuesday and Friday nights and it was usually Van, Bob Werner and myself. You had mentioned that you spoke with Bob McAdoo earlier…I remember this one time we were playing a couple exhibition games up in Toronto…four exhibition games and it was on a Sunday and after the games Ernie "D" came walking out of the locker room with his Navy Pea coat on and his gloves were pinned to his sleeves and my wife asked Ernie why do you have those pinned to your sleeves and he said that his wife would yell at me if I lost them. Ernie I said, they only cost .45 cents… yea well she'll still yell at me if I lost them.

There were some strange times with Van. I can tell you that I saved Van any number of times from taking a head first dive out the press box window out at the stadium. We'd be doing a game and he'd get so excited that he'd jump up on the table of the booth and lean out the window shouting this, that and the other. The fans would go nuts but he'd often go a bit to far and almost fall out the window so I would have to grab the back of his pants and drag him back inside the booth.

The window of the booth was always open we never closed it regardless of the weather because we wanted to get the sense of the crowd during that particular game we were calling. Despite the weather and the times he was sick Van never missed a game ever during his career and he was pretty sick at times...regardless of his health he never missed a game. There was this one time both Van and Murph had cups of water in front of them because they talked to so much and one time it was so cold that Murphy's water had frozen but we always opened the windows about fifteen minutes before game time. There's this other time and perhaps I shouldn't say but one time in the middle of a game Van gets this gash across his head and the blood is dripping down. I always had a stack of napkins with me just incase and this moment was definitely a just incase moment. Van was still trying to call the play as I'm tugging back on his forehead and stemming the flow of the blood...we managed to hold him back and Murph finished the next couples of plays while we patched Van up.

You know Van has been out of the spotlight for a number of years now...five at least and so a goodly number of folks aren't familiar with him but I remember not long ago we were in a restaurant and this young boy comes up to Van and says hi Mr. Miller it's nice to meet you. So Van reaches into his wallet pulls out a dollar hands it to the boy and thanks him for the compliment. He just thought that was so cool. Van I don't think has an enemy in the world. I don't think that anyone can say anything bad about Van and that doesn't happen much anymore because it seems that everyone has an enemy deservingly so or not. The more a person may be a professional threat than perhaps the greater the "enemy" they will be.

There have been many games that will always stand out as remarkable or memorable and the first Super Bowl in Tampa is one...wide-right that should have been our game there are many stories about those and some I can't say but as far as Van I never saw anyone work so hard as he did during those Super Bowl games. He worked fifteen, sixteen hour days or even more. He was always telling us no go to dinner...take Gloria to dinner he had work to do and he always kept his own calendar...he never had a personal assistant. Van kept his own appointment book. There may have been an agent a few years ago when there was that movie made, Second String with Jon Voight…it could be about this time that he was required to join a union and they required an agent. I don't think Van ever made use of that.

If Van could say one thing about the fans I am sure he would say he loved them. He was cordial to everyone and he always went over to everyone and said hello or had his pictures taken with the. I think that Van is remembered for his good-hearted natured…his friendliness and for not having an enemy. Van is the voice…he is the face for the Buffalo sports scene. There will never be another Van Miller and like Don Paul said he is unique in a world when that word is hard to define.

Dr. Bob Werner

Rob I haven't used Doctor in years, professionally I was a dentist but Van made me more famous than what my career did…at the end of each game always crediting me with…and on stats Dr. Bob Werner.

How long were you Van's stats guy?

I was his statistician for many years, the exact number I can't be sure. I don't think I was terribly good at it either. I always crossed this out and that out. I was always off by a couple of yards here and there too. I still have the stat sheet that I used during the comeback game against the Oilers. I had it framed and gave it to my grandson.

That had to be quite a day to keep stats.

Oh man I can't tell you it was something else. You undoubtedly heard this many times by now Rob but that first half that day couldn't have been any worse for the Bills and when they, the Oilers came right out after half-time and scored again of a Frank Reich interception the stadium nearly emptied out. The numbers were horribly lopsided. Warren Moon had over two hundred yards and four touchdowns in the first half and I clearly remember the Bills had the ball for less than ten minutes; they couldn't do anything with it. Frank had replaced Jim Kelly and when he had thrown that interception which was returned for a touchdown it was suddenly 35-3 and the stadium emptied but we all know what happened after that.

I was in college in Memphis at the time so I was one of the few who can say I actually watched it on television. It was televised everywhere except the Buffalo area.

There are not many who can say they saw the game on TV and even a smaller number can say they were in the stadium and hung around 'till the very end. Probably a hundred thousand would say they were there that day now after the fact.

Let's start from the beginning though, how long have you known Van?

Oh let's see I've know him since I was a young man…Pearl Harbor Day was in 1941 and I was going down to Dunkirk at the time so I would say I have known Van for sixty-eight years at least.

Since you were both teenagers in other words?

Yes…well I was a year or two younger than he was. Van knew my cousin pretty well, they were friends and every summer I'd go down to Dunkirk and spend a couple of weeks with my cousin and his family so that's how I got to know Van. As a matter of fact the first time I ever met him I was swimming in Lake Erie and I came up from under water and sprayed a moth full of Erie right in his face…that was our first meeting so to speak.

But I really got to know him well or better when I was of high school age. My cousin's family had a farm on the lakeshore and they, my cousin and Van, played together all the time and when I came down in the summer it was like we picked up right where we left off the previous year, our first meeting was I guess you say by chance.

What was Van like as a teenager?

Well I'm sure you have heard many stories but you have to know that even as a young man Van was quite gregarious already. He was very out going and everyone liked him. He loved to play sports and from what I learned he was interested in broadcasting early on in life. He was very friendly to everyone. When I first met him it wasn't like I was a stranger it was like I had always been his friend.

That does seem to be a common element with everyone I have talked to but I have found out too that Van is a very private person as well.

Yes he is, but in public he is a superstar. He was so well known all over the country and I saw it first hand but in those early days in Dunkirk I had heard more about him.

A person's reputation often tells more about a person than the person can say for himself or herself and often that is very unfair but in his case I don't think he has an enemy in the world or is there a person who can say anything disparaging about him. If they do, it must be out of some form of professional jealousy. But again Rob I didn't know Van well during his early years. I'd have to say again that I really got to Van best after he and Gloria moved to Buffalo and we became neighbors. We lived only a couple of streets apart and were in easy walking distance to each other's homes and we'd begin to chat on walks or we'd both attend a neighborhood event.

This was in the '60s and Van and I were in the same social circles so we got reacquainted again with, to a degree the memories of Dunkirk serving as a conversation starter and it didn't take long for us to pick up right where we had left off as teenagers. We developed a great friendship and in a short time he'd start taking us to Bills games and so that's where I first met "Dobby", Ralph Hubbell was there as well and Ed Gicewicz was with Van so that's where I say I got to know him best was during his early broadcast days with the Bills. The Dunkirk days, he was not a shy kid by any means. Dunkirk wasn't a big place so everyone knew everyone else and we all hung out together even though I was there only during the summer I felt like I fit in. When the '60s rolled around that's where we got to know each other much better. When Van and Gloria moved to the area my practice...my dental practice was in full swing so I became their dentist and I got to appreciate his children and he and Gloria got to know our family.

You worked for him from the AFL days on?

Yes I did. I'm sure Van has told you this but going to a Bills game back then was a pretty simple process, it was a painless activity and when game day came we'd leave our homes about 11 or 11:30 even though Van was working the game and we'd get there still in plenty of time. Now going to a game is a daylong adventure, now we have to leave at 10 and perhaps get home by 7 or even later. 'The Rockpile' was a much simpler stadium, there were no parking lots so you had to park on adjacent streets or you know in the front yards of the home owners who charged a couple of bucks for the privilege. Back then you knew everyone too and you'd get into a routine and week after week you would have the same spot and say hi to the same people and we always got out and got home in time. Early on his cousin's husband Jimmy helped him a great deal by being his yardage guy and he in turn taught me what I needed to know about doing stats.

"The Rockpile" was a very primitive environment as far as stadiums go, there the field…the stands and the restrooms it was all quite primitive. The hot dog concessions was like a little frying pan and some old lady from the cities public works department used to come cook for us and for awhile I used to be the hot dog guy…you know getting hot dogs for everyone. The press box was probably 25x20 it was a big box compared considering what there is now and Van would take as many people as possible with him there.

The press box had more space because of the lack of engineers and producers that there is now don't you think?

Well from what I recall there were three people with him. Three would be enough to do a good broadcast and Van would have all of us doing a separate job and he'd have someone doing yardage and another keeping track of punts and so on. Van would prepare most of his own charts and they were really good and of course he studied the players during the course of the week incessantly. He really knew most of the players cold especially the Bills and with the number of times we played other teams he got to know the opponents quite well too. So because of his preparation his broadcasts in the beginning were excellent. Van could inject a lot of emotion too because he knew everything so well and was just tremendously gifted at what he did.

We see so many announcers today, at least I do and you said you have too Rob, who are bad in the broadcast booth. They might be bad for any number of reasons but lack of practice might be the main reason. Van, his emotion was infectious and he was so well know nationally for how he called a game and I didn't realize just how ell know he was until he'd take me to a couple of road games and would walk me through the press box and introduce me to all these people in the field. He was known tremendously across the nation and greatly respected as well. Whoever called him a rock star of broadcasting was correct Van was the guy; he was the personality here in Buffalo. The Bills games of course he did but when the season was over he was still just as busy. He did his sportscasts of course but he did Niagara University basketball games and after WBEN lost the Bills contract he did every single one of the Buffalo Braves NBA games. I don't think he ever missed one of those. He did bowling shows, quiz shows, Van was everywhere and everyone loved him. What the readers should know though is that Van is a very loyal friend.

Loyalty seems to be a family trait. Did you know his mother?

Yes I knew his mom quite well. Van is dedicated to his friends and he was very loyal and dedicated to his mother. His mother held a special spot for him. I remember that he'd often drive down to Dunkirk to take her to Mass. Folks should know that Van would do anything for anyone. He loves people and people love him.

Mike Mullane

I grew up knowing John Murphy and John and I have known each other since we were kids. John, as everyone knows was Van's color man for seven years or so. I think it was in 1989 and the Bills were playing in the Hall of Fame game down in Canton Ohio and John asked if I wanted to go along and join him and Van in the booth and perhaps help with stats a little. I leapt at the opportunity of course. At the time stats weren't computerized as they are now and so you had a big chart in front of you to record everything on. Now the Bills and Jim Kelly were running the 'K-Gun' and everything was really fast and it being my first time I was doing my best to keep up with the pace of the game. That was quite an experience I assure you. When the Bills switched radio stations John wasn't there which meant I wasn't there either but when they went back to the old station I rejoined him and Van. I was thrilled because I was a genuine armchair fan and I was given quite a chance.

After Van asked me to return as a spotter I'd spot for him for the next ten years right through to his last game against the Patriots. I still am a spotter for John and Mark Kelso I have probably done fifteen or twenty away games over the years. I grew up as a fan. John and I listened to Van so getting to do the games with and for him was just a unique experience.

I have to say Rob that there is many little things I remember about Van but one thing I thought was always cool was when after the game the NFL would knock on the door of the booth and ask if Van would come and do a voice over. He had such a unique voice…such a unique style and the league knew it too but regardless it was quite a treat watching Van do NFL Films. He was never a homer of course but he could hold the attention of any fan with his call of the game and certainly with his humor.

There was this one time we were in Cleveland doing a game at the old stadium there on the waterfront and the broadcast booth was virtually on top of the stadium and to get to it we had to walk up this old gangplank looking ramp.

I remember that field it wasn't grass at all it was a hundred yards of dirt.

That's right it wasn't modern by any definition of the word. So we were up in the press box on top of the stadium and we were so high up that he'd say to Murph that he had just seen a 747 go by and he could see what the passengers were having for dinner.

There is this other time too, Van was good at comically throwing his spotters under a bus for instance one time in the middle of a home game Van got a bloody nose and what does a person do when they get a bloody nose…they tilt their head back. Van couldn't very well do that in the middle of his play-by-play so even though I was the spotter I dropped what I was doing and ran around getting napkins to stop the flow of blood, Murph took over the mic for a few plays until we got Van patched up and Van had since said that his spotter Mike Mullane had elbowed him that day.

Van could sell it though, whatever *it* was don't you think?

Sure Van could sell to the listener the game, the play all by his voice and his humor. He was a tremendous salesman for radio. He had tremendous enthusiasm for football or for any for that matter. What he did which probably a lot of people don't realize is that he used to practice making calls before the game using his radio voice and using my name or Murphy's name…and he knick-named me Night Train. Van would start out Night Train Mullane is at the forty, he's at the thirty the twenty oh he fumbles into the crowd. Van would do this a couple of times and he was warmed up for the game.

Rob Van always made me laugh regardless of how lousy the game was and there was some bad football at times. I will always cherish those days and I think if Van had a chance to say something to all the fans he would say thank you for being so loyal for all the years. There has been some success for the Bills but there have been many disappointments too but the fans always stuck by him, they stuck by the team and the stuck by Ralph Wilson through the good and the bad.

As I said Rob I grew up listening to Van and I watched him on television sports and I watched him do the Buffalo Braves so he was whom I admired and getting the chance to work alongside him for those ten years was an incredible honor for me even though I was occasionally thrown under the bus. Van will always be remembered and held close to the hearts of everyone who have come to know him over the last forty plus years.

Art Plant

Rob I didn't come on board with Van until the first Super Bowl in Tampa Bay and that would be in 1991. I was the rookie of the crew. I used to go up to Channel 4 every now and then…let me back up a bit. I was a friend with Carol Jason who worked at Channel 4 at the time. Carol was the first female news anchor at the station and she was like myself a big fan of the Boston Red Sox. Now besides teaching at Kenmore West I had a little business on the side where I'd supply groups and collectors with memorabilia primarily Red Sox memorabilia and the name of my business was 4-Ever Fenway.

So I got to know Carol because of our shared love of the Red Sox and so I would drop an item off at the station every so often for her and this one time I dropped into the station around Christmas time to wish her a Merry Christmas…anyway I'm sitting in the lobby waiting for her to come off the set and while I'm waiting Van walks by. Now Van knows me because he has seen me around the station every now and then but he didn't know I was Art Plant anymore than anyone else knows I am Art Plant. As Van is prone to do he started up a conversation with me a relative stranger and I asked him in the midst of our chat…if the Bills make it to the Super Bowl could he get me a couple of tickets to the game? Van said they would be in Tampa and staying and so and such hotel and to give him a call if I managed to get down there. The Bills did make it to the Super Bowl. I finished up school for Christmas and I took some additional time off as well and went down to Tampa and I did as he asked, I gave him a call.

In Tampa I stayed with a friend in Sarasota and so I called the hotel where Van was staying and he said…check back with me…and these calls went on for a day or two. He did manage to get me two tickets to Super Bowl XXV and the morning of the game we rode with him and Gloria to the stadium. Normally the drive from the hotel to the stadium…The Sombrero would take ten to fifteen minutes tops but that day it was an hour perhaps closer to two hours to get there. The press box was up in heaven and the players looked like large ants from the box. Anyway I went to the game with his family and Dick Dobmeier. A couple of things stick out about that day…one was when we went through security. I was not far behind

Victor Kiam who was the owner of Remington Razor…he was incredibly affronted at having to go through security…it was truly a don't you know who I am moment if there ever was one. The security guard handled it calmly and said that he had a choice to watch the game from the stadium or his hotel.

Some weeks later I mentioned to Van that I'd like to get a chance to see him work a game from the press box and he said no problem what so ever and that he'd be happy to show me around. Well the first game of the following season…the '91 season was against the Dolphins and he called me up and says Art I got a ticket for you if you want to come and see the press box. I did and that morning we had breakfast together and he asked if I would like to record yardage for him…well who wouldn't. I said absolutely…he had a statistician…Dr. Bob Werner so Bob would do the stats on paper and I would do yardage…it was a simple assignment, Bob would keep the stats and let's say there was a pass play from the 29 to 45 I would signal Van 16.

That first game led to the next and the next and after awhile my duties expanded and back then there wasn't the assistance from the NFL like there is now with stats…so we did it all with our hands, minds and charts. Now the NFL has a special website that can be logged onto by members of the media to get instant information…well there is a slight delay but I still provided Van with the information and I would do most of the away games too when Bob Werner did not travel, except the west coast games. Van and I became quick friends and I remained in the box with him until he retired and I still do stats for John Murphy and Mark Kelso.

I guess once I said yes to helping him out at that first game and that was all it took. The experiences and the memories have been something else. I know you have probably heard talked to others about the comeback game but I have to share this with you about that day…January 3rd. Each morning I read a devotional, it's called God's Minute and each day the reading deals with a different topic, love…sin…forgiveness etc. Well that morning was a Sunday I got up and read my devotional and this is what it said:

Precious Heavenly Father, hundreds of miracles happen every day.
Thank you for them today. Help me recognize them and to allow them to happen.
What a day it is going to be!

The Bills had just been beat by Houston a couple of weeks earlier prior to the end of the regular season and they had been beat pretty bad down in Houston. Houston was coming up to Buffalo for the playoff game as a hot team. So the day of the game comes and Van and I our having breakfast together and he is visibly upset. He isn't eating and he is pacing back and forth. He looked like a kid waiting for Christmas to come. I asked him what was bothering him and he said he didn't have a good feeling about the game at all. I told Van to relax and that everything was going to be all right. He wanted how I knew and I said because my morning devotional had reassured me. He said that we would see but he felt the game was going to be a tough one.

The game starts out And Warren Moon is simply picking the Bills apart and of course Jim Kelly went down with strained ligaments in his knee and Frank Reich had been leading the team. At half time we were down by 25 points and Van says to me...Art you know what you can do with that devotional now don't you? I told him Van I know it doesn't look good but don't give up it's not over yet. The second half started and pow right off Frank threw the interception that was returned for a touchdown and now we were down by 32 points. This time Van rips his headset off and I'm sitting on the photo deck...you know the booth is small and when we started working together I used hand signals but as the years went on I began to use a dry erase board and would show that to him from my position on the photo deck. So as I said Van ripped his headset off and yells down to me; Art you better get rid of that damn devotional and try something else because it isn't working!

Well it was at that point when we were down by 32 points that I admitted things didn't look very promising. But you and every other Bills fan and former Oilers fans knows what happened...miracles happen and at their pace not when we want them to happen. I tell you the primary reason the Bills won that game wasn't because the Bills put on a second half offensive show. Warren Moon was the Oilers quarterback and he was a phenomenon. He is one of the few guys who had over four hundred yards passing multiple times in a season but what ultimately did the Oilers in was they couldn't run the ball in the second half. In the second half they couldn't run it, they were going three and out with each possession. The Bills stuffed the running game and they were forced to throw to keep the clock moving and we stopped that too. We got the lead at one point and Moon tied it with a drive for a field goal and Steve Christie of course won it in overtime. In my experiences I think that may have been the only time where Van doubted if the team could win or not.

This is a side note to it all, to that day. I taught school at Kenmore and my classroom was across the hall from an agnostic and of course an agnostic has an answer for everything and I told him the story about the devotional and how it applied to the game. He says well it's a good thing someone in Houston didn't read the same devotional. I couldn't believe it because agnostics and atheists have answers for everything and even on the field after the game God was being prevented, the media was interviewing Frank Reich and Frank begins with…I first want to give praise…he was interrupted by the reporter. Franks say no…I want to give praise to my Lord and Savior Jesus Christ. The game itself was a vehicle for Frank to get the message of miracles out to an audience of millions. The message was that faith in Jesus is the way. It was a fitting opportunity for Frank to witness and for me to see how true my morning devotional was.

Rob I work with Murph now and he has had big shoes to fill but one thing that he has had that Van didn't, with the exception of Ed Rutkowski, was someone with a football background to sit alongside him in the booth. Now there is Mark Kelso for Murph and he's doing a terrific job and prior to Mark was Alex Van Pelt.

Van, he had such a way with words…he wasn't obnoxious, he wasn't like…well like John Sterling is for the New York Yankees…I can say that being a Red Sox fan…Sterling is awful…but Van interjected a positive feel for the home team but he did it in a way where if you weren't a Bills fan you weren't turned off by listening to his broadcast.

Van just used words and phrases that were magical and that's why he in the Hall of Fame and if he hasn't told you Rob he is the only local announcer to be in the Pro Football Hall of Fame…there are national guys like John Madden but Van is the only local guy. I was blessed to have worked with and for Van for a decade…yes I did stats but I also compiled other data and records for example; Jim Kelly just had his fifteenth consecutive completion or Bruce Smith his 150th career sack. There are many fond memories but for me the most enduring is our friendship.

CHAPTER ELEVEN

I don't think there will ever be a group of players
together on one team like we had during those Super Bowl years

One of the most enjoyable parts of our chats with Van was when we talked about the history of the Buffalo Bills. Van quite often down played his part of that history but it was Van who introduced the Bills to the general public when TV wasn't always available. I shared with him the story of when my brother Scott surprised me one Christmas with tickets a Buffalo Bills game...the Bills versus the New England Patriots.

The Patriots of the '70s had some good players with Steve Grogan and Russ Francis...and a...I can't remember who that back was they had...but the Patriots going back to the days when we played them in Fenway always had good players and they always played us hard.

Sam Cunningham was the fullback.

That's right, Bam, Sam 'The Bam' Cunningham. He had huge legs...big calves...he was like...not too much...but he ran like Larry Csonka did. You mentioned some of the Bills of the early '70s...WBEN had lost the contract and I was doing Braves basketball but the Bills regardless of record always seemed to have good...memorable players here.

When you look at the Bills teams of the 1960s...the AFL years...when the Buffalo Bills won back to back championships in '64 and '65 those were the only professional sports championship titles that ever came back to Buffalo. They had some great players...Jack Kemp, Wray Carlton and Mike Stratton. If Mike Stratton had not taken out Keith Lincoln in that game…that title game in 1964 against the San Diego Chargers…the Bills perhaps would have lost that game.

If you remember the Chargers had taken the ball right down the field on one of their first drives of the game…maybe it was the first…but they had taken the ball all the way down field and scored. The Bills were three and out and the Chargers were driving again when Mike Stratton hit Keith Lincoln…really one of the stars of the league at the time. The hit broke a couple of his ribs and knocked him out of the game. The Bills rolled after that. The players of the '60s…The Electric Company and Joe Ferguson of the '70s who is one of the kindest most decent men one can meet all the way through to the teams of today the Bills had some great players but none were better than the teams that went to the Super Bowls.

We can possibly compare a couple of the Super Bowl teams to the '64 and '65 championship teams. After the '64 team took the title the following year, 1965 it was a rematch with the Chargers but it wasn't much of a game. The Chargers were favored again but the Bills shut them out but there has always been some really good players to come through Buffalo. There was O.J. of course. I conducted one of the very first interviews with O.J. after he was signed by the Bills…his original number wasn't 32 as some might think it was 36. Greg McDermott had the number when O.J. was drafted but he was traded before the start of the season.

The 1960's were some great days in professional football as we talked about early on in the book the AFL had won the war against the NFL when Pete Gogolak the Bills place kicker was signed by the NFL Giants and a merger then was inevitable…there were some mean and lean years here and there seemed always to be more of them than good ones. There were always interesting…curious people and one of the most interesting guys working for the Bills at the time was the trainer Ed Abramowski…he raised pigeons…he absolutely loved pigeons.

A little something extra with Ed Abramowski

I have to ask Ed, how long have you been raising pigeons and I guess the follow-up question would be why?

Oh I've been raising pigeons since I was twelve years old a kid down in Erie Pennsylvania so some sixty plus years. I didn't have any when I was in college or when I worked at the

University of Detroit but other wise I have raised them all my life…as soon as we got our own house I got the pigeons back up again.

Just curious and I don't know how to ask…but what I know about pigeons is only from what I see in the parks…so what is it that intrigues you about them?

What intrigues me about pigeons? Well I had an uncle who had them and it's amazing to me when you can take them 600 miles away and they'll fly for fifteen hours and come right back home…right back to your backyard. The ones I have are racing pigeons and when I started my birds here in Buffalo we had I think about 120 guys who would race them and now we have about…oh maybe 15 or 18 guys left. It's a dying sport here in Buffalo but in places like California and other places along the East Coast it's a thriving sport and everybody now they have GPS. With that you have the exact mileage and let's say you let them go in Erie Pennsylvania which is approximately 100 miles and you have the exact measurements from your home to there. So let's say a guy in Amherst flew 110 miles and I flew mine 100 miles and the pigeons flew 60 miles an hour that's a mile a minute and he clocked at 11:10 I would have to clock at 11:00 to beat him and so that's how it works. The wind determines a lot when it comes to pigeons. Here in Buffalo the wind comes primarily out of the southwest when you have good pigeons you can overcome wind concerns…my birds are all pedigree too…you know just like horses…I can trace some of them back to 1890.

Van had mentioned it to me and I was frankly quite curious. You came to the Bills pretty much right from the start of their first season.

That's right I worked for the University of Detroit and I was also the game day trainer for the Detroit Lions and Mr. Wilson knew of me. I was introduced to him a couple of times. I didn't really know him well but he hired the Lions defense coordinator Buster Ramsey to be the Bills first coach. Buster was widely given credit for devising the 4-3 defense and for being the first to blitz a linebacker…anyway Buster had been with the Lions for seven or eight years and Mr. Wilson who was from Detroit hired Buster to be the Bills first coach. So Buster asked me to come along because he knew what I could do and I didn't have to be watched in making sure the job got done. What was good was the University of Detroit played either on Friday or Saturday and the Lions played on Sunday so I could do both and I was always free for the home games on Sundays. At that time I was the youngest trainer at a Division one school, the University of Detroit. Remember during that time...the '50s anyway the Lions had some really good players...Bobby Lane...Doak Walker and Yale Lary of course who finished up with the Vikings. In the years that I was there which was '56 to '59 Bobby Lane was still there with Tobin Rote as his backup Bobby Lane.

You came to the Bills because of your familiarity with Buster Ramsey the Bills first coach?

Yes sir, Buster knew I knew what I was doing and that I had a good amount of experience at both the major college and professional levels so that would be one less headache for him...you know an experienced trainer.

I had an opportunity long ago to work briefly for Jack Kemp how well did you know him?

Oh I knew Jack about as well as anyone I guess...he and I were great friends and I kept in touch with him all the time when he was in Washington. He and I were at different ends of the political spectrum but he'd always ask my opinion on different things. I grew up in Erie Pennsylvania, which was a union town and my dad worked in the steel mills and my mother, was a Democratic committeewoman for twenty years so I was a Democrat, a born and bred Democrat and Jack was a Conservative, a born and bred Conservative. But Jack would poll me on different things...what do I think of this and what did I think of that but I regardless of political parties I always voted for him every time he ran...even for Vice-President. It would have been nice to call the White House and say hey man fix this or fix that. He was a true, true guy and great friend and he believed in what he was doing. My mother told me that to be elected to anything you have to be in the middle of the bell shaped curve you couldn't be to far to the right or to far to the left. He was genuinely for the little guy...he was important in the fight for league integration. Jack had come from a family who did it on their own so his belief was that everyone could do it on their own. I remember that he gave me the book...The Rise and Fall of the Roman Empire...he gave me that book forty years ago and now...well take a look at all the things that are happening now in the country. I think he may have known the course we'd be heading down.

He too was one of the very few quarterbacks to have lifted weights. He worked out everyday in the gym and on the weights and not just for a few minutes but he did it rigorously. I remember one thing that he told me…back in those days…the '60s the teams didn't call the defensive schemes…there were no defensive coordinators so to speak. So for the Bills it was Harry Jacobs who called the defensive schemes and Harry was right on with all his calls and in Jack's opinion Harry Jacobs is probably was one of the most underrated players in Bills history…perhaps league history. He was very good at what he did…he never missed a game and he never missed a practice and he never got hurt.

He was probably much sicker than he let on.

I was shocked that Jack passed so quickly. He always took tremendous care of himself and he always had the city of Buffalo in his heart…he loved Buffalo…that I knew and that he showed. He was an ambassador for the city…like Tim Russert and I think too much like Van was and is.

I have heard that from many people…that Van was seen as an ambassador for the city of Buffalo. What would say is the memory you have that sticks out more than any other about that first season with the Bills?

Well it was all that we had to go through just to put a team together…we had so many guys in camp…probably 120 or 130 to start off with. They were college guys…NFL guys and Canadian league guys all looking to extend their career a little longer…un-drafted guys…you know the walk on types too everyone and anyone because they all saw the AFL as another opportunity to continue their careers and to play for a couple more years while making some decent money. Another thing that folks may not know or remember is that the uniforms were a carbon copy of those worn by the Detroit Lions, they weren't the Bills uniforms or even close to the ones they have now.

That's right the team had silver helmets.

Yup…Honolulu blue jerseys and silver helmets. That was our uniform I remember we were supposed to have some Detroit guys with us…coaches and executives of some sort but I guess we got their uniform colors instead. I remember too that Buster always had a disdain for college coaches because so many of the college coaches were saying that they were the ones who trained professional football players and all the pro coaches had to do was line 'em up and play them…Buster of course didn't care for those remarks very much and every time we'd play a former college coach who had come to the pros and we'd beat them Buster would always say…take a suck of that college coach.

We all came on at the same time. Buster and I and Van too and one of the things I remember about Van is that whenever we played a California team he'd be the first one pool side…I think he changed his clothes in a phone booth. He must have kept his swim trunks on under his suit. He was always ready for the diving board when we hit California.

Van though as we have said liked to be kidded by the players and he kidded them back. He fit in when other medias didn't. Van was just a fixture, he was Buffalo to so many of the teams fans outside New York…when someone was asked…when a fan of the Bills who lived somewhere else was asked about what they knew of the Bills they might rattle off a few players but year after year they knew Van was there. He loved what he did and it showed and everyone loves him and they should.

A little more with Ed Rutkowski

Rob in talking about the '60s you can't help but remember Jack Kemp. I think that may be one of the problems with athletes is that we are taught to play through pain and sickness and perhaps he let it go too long. I still have a very hard time in accepting the fact that he's gone.

I guess I do too. He was there any time I called. You came aboard with the Bills in '63?

Yes I was a free agent from Notre Dame and the Bills signed me in 1963 as a player that would do a little bit of everything.

I saw that you were quarterback, kick and punt off returner, receiver, and defensive back…essentially a Steve Tasker of the '60s. When were you at Notre Dame?

I was there from 1959 to 1963 and I received my degree in Political Science. Joe Kuharich was our coach...The Kook...we had some tough years with our best record being 5-5. We had an awful lot of talent but we just couldn't get it going.

There was one game in '61 or '62 against Syracuse and a missed field goal.

Yes it was in South Bend and we were trailing by one point, 15-14 with only a couple of seconds left and we were lining up to kick a long field goal. Joe Perkowski kicked a field goal and Walt Sweeney burst through and knocked the holder and kicker over like they were bowling pins and the official threw the flag. The clock had run out. Syracuse contended that the game was over and under the existing rules another free kick couldn't be allowed. Well the fifteen-yard penalty was enforced and we were allowed another kick. The kick was good and we won the game. The rule change that came as a result of this game was a half could not end on a defensive penalty. A lot of folks thought it was me who was the kicker Perkowski...Rutkowski and we were both from Wyoming Valley so it was nice to have been remembered for something positive like that.

Wasn't there also a mess up on your Topps football card too?

Yea they did mess it up they had one of my cards with Ray Abruzzese's name on it.

Well it's understandable your names sound so much alike...Abruzzese and Rutkowski.

Sure they do don't they?

Rob we had so many players coming and going in the early years. I made the Bills as a cornerback...imagine a slow kid from Notre Dame making the team as a cornerback but I did. I played that position my first year and then we had a series of injuries and I was switched over to halfback and I played there for a couple of years. Then if they needed me at wide receiver I played that and in my last year we had injuries at quarterback with both Jack Kemp and Tom Flores going down so I started the last part of the season at quarterback. Which I really enjoyed because I did always wanted to play quarterback.

1968 was not a good year.

It was 1-12-1 the one win coming against Joe Namath and the Jets...we had two head coaches that year...Joe Collier and Harvey Johnson. No the year wasn't a good one.

Playing for the O.J. pick?

Well I was the guy...that's my legacy. I was the responsible for getting the Buffalo Bills O.J. Simpson because of my fumble against the Oakland Raiders. It was kind of interesting we had to play Denver on a Sunday and we were beating them until Floyd Little had come out of the backfield for a good pick up and ran out of bounds. They kicked a field goal and beat us by a couple of points. After Denver we had to go to Oakland to play the Raiders on a Thursday afternoon on national television so we didn't get much rest or practice.

We were told that the Raiders weren't going to take us seriously and it was likely that they'd use only three or four standard defenses and we had set offensive plays for each of those defenses and I carried this play book with me every where I went. It was my Bible that week and it's amazing because I audiblelized about fifty percent of the time during that game and we almost beat them...we lost 13-10. We had a field goal that bounced off the crossbar and then we got down to their two or three yard line and I called a naked reverse and I fooled everyone except George Atkinson who reached around and knocked the ball out of my hands and recovered it.

So if I had scored that touchdown we would have won the game and not been in a position to draft O.J. Now I still kid Ralph Wilson all the time I tell him that he owes me a finder's fee for being the one responsible for bringing O.J. to Buffalo. Ralph always says no though. Well actually Ralph actually says is that he was on the sidelines that day and Harvey Johnson was our coach at the time and Harvey asked Ralph well what do you want to do kick a field goal and tie it or go for the win...Ralph said go for the win and give the ball to Rutkowski and let him run it in. Well the end result was a fumble and O.J. Simpson coming to the Buffalo Bills. Ralph said that he was ultimately responsible for O.J coming because he let me run it...he's the boss. I knew my career was coming to an end I thought I could play another couple of years but I was at the point where it would be one year with one team and another somewhere else so I said no to that because I didn't want to move my family around but I did go up to Montreal and played one year with the Alouettes of the CFL.

When did you get interested in politics?

Well at the time Jack and I lived in Hamburg and we'd ride together to practice and I always knew that when he was done with football that Jack would get involved in politics. During the off-season he worked for different groups and made political speeches and when he retired he wanted me to work for his campaign and I thought it was tremendous opportunity. I ran his volunteer campaign and he won the Congressional seat with 51% of the vote. It was a tough race but he kept the seat for a generation.

One of the thoughts we had initially was that why does a football player think he ought to run for Congress. So we tried to get Jack out to as many coffee klatches and meetings as we could to show just how articulate he was on the issues. That was important because in that first race our opponent was Thomas Flaherty an Irish Catholic widower with four or five kids and he would be tough to beat.

I hope that Jack will be remembered for many things but one thing that should never be forgot is that he was a head of a union himself he was the first players union president. I remember that when Bethlehem Steel was still here we'd be down at the gates first thing in the morning doing what we could to educate the workers on Jacks own labor background. I'll never forget this either, one time we had Ronald Reagan in town and across from the hall all the union members were protesting one thing or another and it was a cold day...so President Reagan said let's give them some coffee and doughnuts and that's what they did. Ronnie and Jack went and took care of the union members there and it was quite a way to diffuse a situation.

When did you first get to know Van?

If you were a Buffalo Bills fan you were a Van Miller fan. He was the voice of the Bills for some many years and I did have the privilege of being his color man for one year in 1990. Van was the consummate broadcaster and he had a unique ability to paint with words the scene...the play that was taking place on the field. He had a tremendous command of the English language and used words magnificently to describe what was going on, on the field. He made up words of his own that should be in the dictionary and I remember Van always saying it's not what you say it's when you don't say it.

It's when you don't say it?

Yea it was his way of saying let the crowd report the game…in other words it wasn't important for an announcer to shout and scream when a big play occurs let the crowd tell the story. The crowd will tell the moment and so I learned a lot from Van in knowing when to speak and when not to speak. Van held a lot close to his chest but he did have some of the same jokes that he over and over but regardless of how old the humor was Van is one of the all time great broadcasters. He had such a unique ability and extraordinary talent to make the game so much fun and so memorable even if the season stunk. Van was fare and honest and incredibly friendly with everyone he ever met. He will be remembered as one of the greatest voices the NFL has ever had.

Van with O.J. in his original number 36.

---

*Note: In 1968 number 32 was worn by Greg McDermott…he was traded in 1969 to Atlanta in when O.J. was drafted and O.J. then had number 32.

Rob I was one of the first to interview O.J. Simpson after the Bills had drafted him. He was tremendous at least on the field. We had lost the contract during those years, his years but as a fan I knew what I was watching. Here is another story about a road trip.

Van with O.J. Simpson and Al Cowlings, courtesy of Steve Cichon.

"My $6.00 room courtesy of Mickey Rooney."

Rob have I told you about my first hotel room in Las Vegas? I have to tell you this one before we go much further…it is a true story too. We were on our West Coast swing one season and had just played a game in Los Angeles against Jack Kemp and the Chargers. Barron Hilton owned the team originally and a couple of years later he moved them down to San Diego and they became the San Diego Chargers…the team we all now love and adore.

Anyway after we played the Chargers I remember we were then to go up to Denver and to get to Denver we'd have to fly through Las Vegas. It was 1960 or so and there weren't as many direct flights as there are today and besides it was my first time in Las Vegas. In 1960 we were to fly commercial from L.A.X into Las Vegas. I was waiting to get on the plane and I saw Mickey Rooney saying good-bye to his wife…which one…which wife I don't remember. I got on the plane and I took my seat in first class and Mickey Rooney and his manager sat across from me and so we started up a conversation. We spoke about football and he said he loved the game and thought the new American Football League was a tremendous league and would really make it when all was said and done.

I told him that I had never been to Vegas before and he said he was doing a show at The Flamingo that night and that I could be his guest at dinner and that he'd get me a room for only $6.00. He insisted though that if I'd never been to Vegas before that I should stay at The Stardust and see the Lido Show, which was a copy of the show that they had in Paris. Mickey Rooney said it was fantastic with ice-skating and swimming on the stage it was full of beautiful women and he said if I stayed at The Stardust that I could get a room and you could get into the show too so I did...I stayed at The Stardust. Mickey Rooney had given me a ride into town and dropped me off at The Stardust and from what I recall it was the largest resort hotel of its kind in the world with some 5,000 rooms.

I walked up to the front desk and told the guy I wanted a nice room so I asked how much were they? He said I can give you a room for $6, $7, $8, $9 or $10, and they were also called a Ten Room, A Jack Room, Queen, King and Ace style of rooms. I asked how much the Ace Room was and he said it was $14 but he recommended that I take the $6 or the Ten Room they were about the same all I needed to do was to walk a bit further to the casino, so my first ride into Las Vegas came courtesy of Mickey Rooney and my first hotel room was only $6.

***

So back to O.J. when he was drafted it took a year or two but he turned things around in Buffalo. Lou Saban returned and was going to build a running game around O.J. like he had done with "Cookie" Gilchrist in the '60s. The offensive line had to come together first slowly and via the draft and trades but Ralph Wilson was able to build that offensive line into one of the all-time greats...The Electric Company...Joe Delamielleure is in the Hall of Fame. The quarterback Joe Ferguson was always one of the nicest most down to earth people in the game.

The '90s though...I don't think there will ever be a group of players together on one team like we had during those Super Bowl years...it was incredible. Look at the list...Jim Kelly Hall of Fame...Thurman Thomas Hall of Fame...Bruce Smith Hall of Fame ...James Lofton Hall of Fame...Cornelius "The Biscuit" Bennett...Darryl Talley...Kent.

Van... I hate to interrupt you but may I tell a story? Its involving Darryl Talley.

Sure I love stories Darryl is a great guy...helluva' linebacker now having said that, what did he say about me?

Well I spoke to Darryl about a year ago and I asked him if he had any memorable stories about you… he said, "Van Miller! Oh man have I got story to tell you about Van.

We were in the middle of one of Super Bowl years and it was towards the end of the season…maybe the last home game and we'd clinched the division. I know there was snow everywhere up there that I remember and after the game Van comes into the locker room dragging this large Hefty trash bag behind him. Everyone is looking at him and he walks right up to my locker. I was watching him closely you know because Van could have just about anything in the bag.

He said Darryl I have something for you…so I watched him even closer. What could Van possibly have for me that he was carrying around in a garbage bag?

Darryl I have this fur coat for you and I want to get rid of it so I'll let you have it for only a hundred bucks…back then Rob I used to wear these big fur coats…everyone remembers that I think…it was kinda' my thing. So Van opens this bag and he pulls out this big ol' coat, it was fur alright…I couldn't tell if it was bear or a bunch of rabbits or what…I said Van I have a million coats and besides your name is already embroidered on the outside of this one…his name was in big bold letters. He wanted to sell me a bear coat with Van embroidered on it…now wait it gets better…this is how the rest of the story goes…as far as I remember that day evolving. So Van leaves the stadium without making a sale and he gets into his car and heads back to his home…it was getting dark and it had started to snow again and by now he was wearing this bear coat.

So Van is driving home and he is making his way down one of the side streets close to where he lives…it's dark…the snow is falling and he stops his car…and from what I was told about what happened next he gets out of his car because lying out in the middle of the road was this golden lab. Van knew it was his neighbors' dog so he gets out goes over and scoops the dog up and puts it into the passenger side of the car. Van then drives over to his neighbors house and goes up and knocks on the door…Mrs. Brown or whoever comes out and says…Hi Van what can I do for you…Van proceeds to say; I have found your dog lying out in the middle of the road so I picked it up and it's in the front seat of my car. The woman looks at him…you got our dog? Is that what you said? Van says yes I have your dog.

Well the woman at that point says Van come here…come inside. Look…what is that laying under our dining room table? I don't know what that is you have in your car but our dog has been inside all day. So Van Miller had apparently dog napped someone's dog and more he did it dressed as a bear. I couldn't imagine what those neighbors thought when they saw this bear swallow up a lab and then get in a car and drive off.

I asked Darryl…was this fact or fiction? Maybe a little of both he said through a chuckle.

Well…is it fact or fiction Van?

Well…I don't know may be a little of both. Darryl was a tremendous ball player…a pretty good storyteller too but this is how that day really went.

I didn't want a hundred bucks for the coat that's not true. I wanted to give it to him because it was so heavy for me to wear but it didn't fit him so that ended that. I will tell you this and Darryl alluded to it. It was during the blizzard of '77 and I woke up in the morning and the Sinclair's up the street had already cleared their driveway. Gloria had some frozen crab in our freezer and wanted to make some Crab Louis Salad but she needed some Mayonnaise and there was a New Way Market open so I would need to make a store run.

I put the bear coat and I got in my little Camero and I started down the road for the New Way Market and who's lying in the middle of the road but the Sinclair's dog Penny she was a 13-year-old Golden Lab. So anyway she was in the middle of the road, it was freezing and I said this dog is going to die of exposure so I got out of the Camero wearing this bear coat. I got the dog to get into the car and I drove over to the Sinclair's house and I go up to the door and rang the doorbell. I was very proud of myself because I had saved their dog from a chilling death. Mary Ellen Sinclair had come to the door. She wanted to know what I was doing out in that weather especially wearing that coat. I said you are going to be glad to see me. She wondered why she was going to be glad to see me. Well because I just saved your dogs life that's why. What are you talking about she asked. I said I have Penny out in the car right now. She said Van get in here for a minute. I walked in and looked under the dining room table and sure enough Penny was there. I had in deed dognapped the wrong dog. I have always been thankful that the rightful owner of that dog didn't have a shotgun when he saw a bear drive off with his dog that morning.

***

I kidded them and they kidded me and to a degree it was almost expected. It was such an incredible period of time for the Bills during those Super Bowl years and even a couple of years before and a year or two after the last of the Super Bowls...the atmosphere before each game was something else. Inside and outside the stadium...outside in the parking lots there was probably as much if not more fun going on than in the stands. It was a perfect match I'd say...in a lot of ways...the players we had they weren't filled egos. They never turned away from an autograph or a photo and even me, even today I get asked if people could take my picture and like then I always say I want my picture taken with you. It might seem ol' fashion to say but we were a giant family and still are. The reunions bring us back together and those guys from the Super Bowls they get the loudest applause. But it can't be forgotten that they didn't all come together accidentally. They were supposed to be together for the time they were here and to bring to Western New York the excitement they did...a lot of fun...a lot of stories and a lot of fur coats.

...Was this the coat?

...Or was it this one pictured here with John Daly?

Those players, sometimes all that has to be said is a number 12 or 34 and a fan will say Kelly or Thurman or say a knick name like "Biscuit" or "House" and they will know who you are referring to.

I think history will eventual confirm that there will never be another group of players of such incredible talent to be on one team for such an extended period of time like they were. Kent Hull was one of the best centers ever... "House" Ballard...and Steve Tasker...one of the best Special Team players ever to play the game. Football historians will be the official judges of such things but the fans are the ultimate judges when it comes to those Super Bowl teams. In the '60s Dick Gallagher was the brain child who put those teams together...but the Super Bowl teams again look at the names and the members of the Hall of Fame on that team that team was put together by Bill Polian now with the Indianapolis Colts and from what I understand Frank Reich is now Peyton Manning's quarterback coach. Polian is, in the minds of many football people a genius...a draft and trade genius but he too was hired by Ralph Wilson...without Ralph Wilson we...Buffalo would not have had the Super Bowl teams.

CHAPTER TWELVE

Vic, you cut me off again…Lou, fire that guy!

Friday, June 5th 1998

WIVB Channel 4 had just celebrated its 50th anniversary, and in all likelihood, the news on that particular Friday would have focused on the restructuring of the municipal government by Mayor Anthony Masiello, or it could have been the still very fresh Northern Ireland Peace agreement, or even the rumblings and rumors surrounding President Bill Clinton and a young intern. But for many in the Western New York viewing audience that night, *that* broadcast would mark an end of an era.

Jacquie Walker

I had graduated from Michigan State University with a degree in Advertising Management and had done well enough so as to be recruited by The Leo-Burnett Agency out of Chicago. They are one of the largest advertising firms in the world, (The Leo Burnett Agency is responsible for the creation of such product icons as The Jolly Green Giant, Charlie The Tuna and Tony The Tiger). It wasn't long, though, before I realized that the world of advertising wasn't for me, and one day, after working there for a couple of years, I walked in and quit even though I had no other job waiting for me. I spent a period of time in self-reflection, trying to figure out what I would do with my life. I was interested…always interested in current events, and like many others, when Walter Cronkite was on in our house…no one spoke…so combining various factors led me to choose broadcast journalism, and I returned to school at Columbia College also in Chicago. I had found that that was the right choice for me, and in a relatively short period of time, I had my first job at a very small, mom and pop station in Springfield Illinois, which has since gone dark.

After some time there, I moved up to the CBS affiliate, WROC, in Rochester and in 1983 came here to WIVB. That's when I first got to know Van. He was by then already well entrenched as a legend. I have been here at WIVB for twenty-six years now, so I worked with Van for fifteen years. I married the most wonderful man on earth and have raised our boys here. I have had opportunities, but western New York is a terrific place to live and to raise a family…but it was in 1983 when I first met Van Miller. Right from the very beginning, I admired the way Van worked. I know he had to have studied scripts or stats, but I never saw him do it. What I saw was his precise use of timing and impeccable, concise use of the language. He was a true master at that. His wit was natural, as well, and there may be many people who would say Van used the same jokes over and over. Well he did, but they never got old to me and they were always fresh and always worked on the person who met him for the first time. I know you have heard this one over and over again, but the line about the earring…it was definitely old, but it worked every time he used it on an unsuspecting woman.

Van always had a twinkle in his eye…I haven't talked to him in awhile now, but I'm sure it's still there. He had the same twinkle in his voice too, and that had to come across during his broadcast of the Bills games.

But sometimes you may not have known what he may have been thinking. There was one night…it was a Halloween night, and we were doing our 6 p.m. newscast. Now, Buffalo, as in all cities have this section of town that is high end…fancy homes and yards…big cars, and here in Buffalo, it's always said to be the Lebrun area of Amherst. Now, Van was finishing up his segment on this one Halloween night, and he said, "Now all you kids—you make sure you go trick-or-treating over on Lebrun because they're giving away free VCRs tonight". Uhg! We all laughed and swallowed hard all at the same time, but Don or I emphasized the importance of the children staying in their own neighborhoods so to prevent a mad rush of cars heading to Amherst. When working with Van, it was important always to be on your toes because of that twinkle.

It was so obvious that Van loved people…he'd stop and talk to anyone…he never carried that do-you-know-who-I-am personality…fans loved him, and he certainly loved them. He also loved the work that he was doing, and he was an absolute consummate professional at what he did. Long before I had started here, Van had been the voice of Buffalo He had done so much and such a variety of broadcasts that he mastered being a broadcaster. He was so quick…he was so concise, and as I mentioned too Rob, he was never fazed by anything. He was the quintessential broadcaster and never seemed to be phased by anything…except perhaps when Don Paul went over his allotted time. That was very real. Van worked hard on his segment and having to cut it short upset him, so the tension between him and Don was real. It was never ugly or taken to a more public level, and Van, with his style, just turned it into a humorous relationship…but he was genuinely upset.

Van was always the consummate professional when it came to his work. His comfort level behind the microphone was something I had not seen…it was natural. The years surrounding the Bills Super Bowl teams, Van may have been at his best. He had waited so long for that opportunity, and he delivered like no ones else I think could. The excitement around the city was incredible, as those of us who were here can remember very well. I was the only news reporter to cover all four Super Bowls…all the others were sports reporters. The sports stories were easy to get…there was always an interview of some type that could be obtained, but my job was to report it as a news event…talking to fans, etc. That was a challenge at times.

Van was the voice, though, and that's what he'll be remembered for. I remember on his last night at WIVB…his last sports cast; we all knew that we were saying good-bye to a legend. My husband and boys were with me that night at the studio…because when Van said good-bye, we knew history was being made. Everyone was there…Van's wife Gloria and the people who had worked with him during the Bills broadcasts. We had a nice celebration for him. Van was given four or five minutes that night to say good-bye…he took his shot at Don Paul…he said thank you for all the years and that was it. There is so much that Van should be remembered for: his work within the community, his charitable efforts and all the lives he has touched with his voice, but it cannot be overlooked that he has had tremendous support for what he did…his mother…he was dedicated to her and Gloria his wife…she has been with him for nearly sixty years and supported him all the way. God most certainly should bless Gloria.

Don Postles

I have been in broadcasting…television news for over thirty years, very close to forty years now. I began at a station in Dayton, Ohio, where Phil Donahue was doing his show. I graduated from American University in Washington, DC and actually ran Howard K. Smith's teleprompter when I was in college. That was the time of World News Tonight or

ABC Nightly News with Howard K. Smith and Harry Reasoner. That was a nice opportunity for me.

I came to Buffalo on Memorial Day, 1976, and I have been with WIVB since 1993…having worked for both GRZ and WKBW prior to coming to Channel 4. Bob Koop was still here when I came, and he had been anchoring various newscasts until John Beard left. I was first a reporter, but within a couple of months, I was anchoring the noon and the 6 p.m. news with Carol Jasen. Then, Bob passed from Leukemia in 2000. I can't quite recall the exact year I became the co-anchor of the noon, 6 and 11 newscasts, but it was Carol, Don and Van.

Though I came to Channel 4 in 1993, I have known Van since 1976. When I was with Channel 7, Van was a fixture in the community…everyone knew him regardless of the station you may have worked for. We seemed to have traveled in the same circles. We worked in television, and it's a small world. Everyone does know each other, so we had many common friends and acquaintances. I would also run into Van in some of the oddest places…at the car wash…at a restaurant or getting his car worked on and one time…when I was at Channel 7, I was doing the 6 and 11 news with Irv Weinstein, and at the time, we were doing the Eye Witness News Game. It'd be my job to go around to the various K-Marts and Target Stores and sign the game for people who wanted to buy the board game. So one day I was up at the K-Mart on Transit Road, and—I'll never forget this—Van Miller was there talking to a guy. Van will talk to anyone…you know this…stranger or life long friend Van will talk to anyone. The guy Van was talking to turned toward me and said…hey, Don Postles! I watch you all the time, and I distinctly remember turning to Van and saying, "Van he's lying to one of us." For some people, Van was a relief after a hard day, and they enjoyed running into him across town.

For Van, being the voice of the Buffalo Bills was his passion. He put so much into he put so much into his sportscasts too, and a great more work goes into that…play-by-play than perhaps people realize…especially in the earl days…the '60s when he first began…gearing up for the game…doing the homework needed for both teams, and he was there during the glory years. He was there during the glory years of the Super Bowl years, and he certainly was there during the bad years…but you know the type of season never affected his broadcast he had the same level of excitement for every game. I can't say he was a homer, but he did it. He broadcast in such a way that he made everyone feel good about the team when things were going well, and I don't believe he offended the non-Bills fans either.

It's all live…so whoever does play-by-play has to be on. You know, I have worked with so many great talents in the thirty-eight years I've been in television, but I will say that Van is the best at adlibbing. He was the best at standing in front of a camera and just talking. He's instant…he's quick there is no doubt whatsoever in my mind that if he gets up in the middle of the night to get a glass of milk and that refrigerator light comes on that he could do two minutes of stand up.

Some of that ability might come from his days of doing early radio, where he had to do everything by himself and he had to be prepared and well thought out for five or six moves ahead, but I think a lot of it comes from his sense of humor. With a quick sense of humor, a person has the innate ability to react mentally and verbally quite well in any circumstance. Now, he may use the same old lines that he's used for years, but they may work as well today as they ever did. If you, or for anyone who has ever heard him emcee a dinner, Van could go on and on and on with stories and tales about one thing and then another. One thing he said to me again and again, "Don I'd rather have a bottle in front of me than a frontal lobotomy." That line never gets stale.

Now jumping ahead to that final night…Carol Jason and I go into the studio…well, first let me back up and say this Van was also the type of guy you could confide in and seek advice from. He was a mentor to many, and he said to me, "Don if you ever get to the point in a newscast where you have to read a name that might trip you up or that might be hard to pronounce…stop just before you get to the name look at it…get it and say it…it will come out near perfect if you give your brain just a moment to absorb it." I used that then, and I use that technique even today. I give Van Miller the credit for giving me some of the best voice coaching I've ever had. I do have to give him credit for that because it has always worked for me.

Now, getting back to the last night…Vans last sportscast. Carol and I go into the studio, and there was no sign of Van. He was in the sports office. I do remember Gloria being in the studio, and the other people there were his spotters for the Bills games…Ed Gicewicz and Dick Dobmeier. They were there with their wives, and Van walked in to the studio just before the sports. He sat down on the set…said this was it and went through it flawlessly as he'd always done and ended it very humbly, saying that it had been an incredible honor to have done what he had done for all the years. He thanked the audience and all of us, and that was it.

There is so much that Van will be remembered for…the early years before I came, but he's a part of Buffalo history. Van will always be remembered for being as the voice of the Bills. He has fans all over the country, and it's because of that. Now, as far as what he has done for the City of Buffalo...that is a more difficult question...he has done so much. He assisted in anyway he could—anyone who asked or he'd emcee the Monday Morning Quarterback Club or serve as a host for charity after charity. I don't know if there was ever a community cause that he ever said no to.

Don Paul

I have been in weather or involved in the broadcasting or teaching of weather for 33 years...beginning with my first on-air assignment in Bangor, Maine and Wichita in 1976. I have many accomplishments that I'm proud of, but I do have one great non-accomplishment I'd like to share: I was personally turned down by Johnny Carson himself for a position as a writer on The Tonight Show. I'll make the story short but...it is interesting now...the head writer wanted to hire me but Johnny vetoed it...twice. At the time, I was writing jokes on the side for a radio personality in New York City, and I had been doing it for a number of years. He always told me that the material I wrote for him reminded him of the material that Carson would do when he and Ed McMahon sat on the couch before Johnny brought out the first guest. This guy in New York said that I should try to get in touch with The Tonight Show and try to do something about it. Well, I didn't give it a second thought 'till I was bored one day while working for a Tampa station when I had noticed that Carson's former writer, a guy named Pat McCormick, had left the show and was doing movies...one was Smokey and The Bandit, and I knew his material and his lines well and I saw that he was now back on the show. So I sent him my material, and he had his secretary send me a note that said he liked what he had read and that he would turn my materials over to the actual head writer of the show.

Well, in a week or so the head writer sent me some stuff...materials that they had used on the show, and he asked me if I could write something like that. I saw an open door, so I churned stuff out and sent it off to New York. Well, this guy gets back to me and says that he loved the material. Johnny hadn't seen it yet, but that he would put it in front of him, and I think he is really going to want to add you to the staff if he is going to add someone. Now, this was '78 or so, and at that time, Carson was thinking of retiring young, so hiring someone new was up in the air. In a couple of weeks, I received a letter saying that Johnny likes your stuff but thought it was too much like Pat McCormick, and he already had one of them. Ok, not a problem.

Now, a couple of years later I had moved to Detroit, and the same writer tracks me down and asks if I still had the material I had previously sent to the show...I did...and he asked me to send it again. He said Johnny would never remember seeing it. Johnny had just signed this huge contract, and he's in a good mood now. So the head writer was going to put my material back in front of Carson for the second time. Well, he did remember it, and was not too pleased in trying to being convinced that it was all new material. So that's my greatest non-accomplishment...being turned down twice by Johnny Carson himself for a position as a writer on The Tonight Show.

Now Uncle Van...we still talk about him pretty often here. John...Murph talks about him all the time...about all the years they worked together in the broadcast booth. It wasn't long ago when John was telling a joke during a commercial break, and before he could get to the punch line, the break ended and his mic was about to turn back on and he never did finish it. I later reminded him of what Van used to do, and Van did this on purpose. He'd be up there on the set with Carol or Jaquie, Bob Koop or Don Postles, and he would purposefully tell a joke knowing the commercial break was coming to an end. He'd begin the joke and then get near to the punch line just as his mic was turned back on after the commercial break, and he'd never get to the punch line. I found this personally hysterical. His timing was impeccable. If he had chosen to do stand up comedy, he could have done that because he knew about every nook and cranny of how people listened and exactly where to time a punch line.

Now, he had some funny little quirks that amused me, and he had or must have had The Great American Song Book, *which contained all the American standards, Gershwin and all but. Van knew the most obscure songs that no one ever recorded, and for some reason, they were stuck in his brain. From time to time, I'd ask him to sing this one about once a year called* The Boulevard of Broken Dreams:

"...The joy you find here, you borrow,
You cannot keep it, long it seems.
But gigolo and gigolette
Still sing a song and dance along
The boulevard of broken dreams..."

He would ham it up and sing this and any of a thousand songs from his vault. He'd ham it up and sing it during commercials breaks and he knew a millions songs like this. Van would always have something new.

I don't think Van has an enemy, but every now and then, he would get mad at me for going over my allotted time. We were given usually three minutes to deliver the weather, and I always came before Van. Sometimes I'd take an extra 15 or 20 seconds, which then had to be taken from Van's time. Van, though, would turn it into this great running gag that he used for twenty years, and whenever he had a speaking engagement, he used me as his foil. I didn't have to be there; he just blamed me. He'd say, "Now that Don Paul. He'd be telling everyone what the temperature is down in Snellingville…or Bumbletown…" Van would pick the most obscure town, and if it was a colorful crowd, he'd get a little more colorful about my weather trivia…but it was never mean. It was just a running gag that existed between us.

Even though there is a fare enough number of years between us, I'm old enough to where Van thought I was a kid. We enjoyed the same music and laughed at the same things, so we did have a common bond. And we really had fun together. I remember once, and it was something meant just for me…there was this one time when he and I had to go to the Erie County Fair and sign autographs at the Channel 4 booth, and he said I could ride with him. Van would drive. Well, we came to the toll booth on the through way, and I started to reach to get the toll money and Van said, "No, no. I got it. Put that away," and he pays the toll. As we pulled away he said, "Buddy boy, you just witnessed history." He did a lot of things just for me, which, as time has passed, I appreciate even more.

I remember his final sports cast with us. The station had given him three or four minutes to say good-bye, and what I have kept as an incredible honor is that Van spent a large portion of that limited time making fun of me. It was stupendous. It was always a running gag between us…the fact that he could use me as a foil all those years…some folks may have believed he meant it, but no…it was a gag, and I can tell you I miss him terribly.

There's this: every now and then, Van would call up and get a forecast, and he called a couple of years ago. We were having a huge lake effect snow at the time, and this particular night, it was snowing hard and he called up…and he said, "Don I have to tell you that Gloria, she is such a wonderful wife…she knows I have a bad back, and she has a bad back, too, and she's out there in the driveway shoveling the snow…" Then Van would yell… and say, "Gloria, I told you not to pile it on the left side of the driveway!" He sets me up and did set me up all the time, has always known that I was a sucker for his jokes and that I enjoyed being one. Yes, Van had some stock jokes, but he was an incredible ad-libber, and if some folks thought he just used the same old storehouse of humor, then they weren't listening very well.

Around here at the station, Van is treated with such esteem and respect that mentioning him or referring back to him as I sometime do is accepted. Generally, the management doesn't allow references to past employees…but not in Van's case. He left on his terms, and he is such an integral part of the station's history and the community that when his name is mentioned people like it. Now…unique is the most overused word in the English language, but Van is unique. His use of the language…his energy level was natural…but it's his voice… his humor, his good-hearted way of living and incredible gracious man, and I miss him a lot.

Vic Baker

Rob I guess I'm one of the old timers around here now. I began as a stringer working for the station out of the Southern Tier in 1971…and as a stringer…which is a free lancer I was young and foolish in some eyes but I went out and covered the floods that happened down there in June of 1972 as a result of Hurricane Agnes.

I grew up in Hornell down in Stueben County and got my start at WLEA a small station down there not far from Alfred University and I covered murder trials, floods, fires etc. from that part of Western New York. I was a student at Fredonia State University at the time and of course I didn't know Van then but I started out by shooting film and they…the station, TV Four would pay me my the piece and they'd pay a little additional if I did the voice over voice over of the story as well. I got to know Van over time by driving back and forth and delivering pieces of film and stories to the station.

I drove it seemed thousands of miles too between Jamestown and Elmira for those floods and I drove thousands more between Hornell, Fredonia and WIVB. I did this until 1975 when the station hired me as a reporter my being familiar with the station and the people and process was awful important to getting that job. I'm also…at least I think I am the only one still here who goes back to the blizzard of 1977 and I was here and fortunate enough to have worked with Van for over twenty-five years and to have produced Van's last broadcast. I was a young guy when I came to the station and getting to see Vans role and influence at the station and in particular the newsroom was great. It was remarkable even more so as I look back from a greater number of years.

Well I came to the station as that stringer in '71 and full time reporter in '75 as I said and Van of course came to the sports desk in '65 replacing Jack Healy but when he first came to the station he was all-purpose…he did everything that could be expected as you have probably discovered by now…there was no tape either so everything was live so if something went wrong it was…oh well move onward and upward.

The thing about Van and his generation of TV announcer is that when they started up it…television was all done live, there was no tape and in the smaller stations they didn't even kinescope…which was a method of recording shows. Now the bigger networks had this method of regarding TV shows but the smaller stations didn't always have this. What they did was basically record the show off a TV screen so that's how some of early TV was saved such as the Honeymooners. Now the local shows such as The Santa Claus Show or Uncle Jerry we didn't have these machines so early television wasn't saved here in Buffalo. Video tape came to the station in '65 and some shows and broadcasts were being saved but the tape was two-inches wide and it was kept on big reels in metal containers so storage space soon became a premium and for that reason the history of early TV in Buffalo much of it anyway has been lost.

The announcers from Vans' generation it was just them and the camera and if things went wrong it was to bad if they let a word slipped or forgot a line they had to stumble through it but by doing and working in that environment. Van learned to think fast on his feet. He learned to talk very concisely and to fill in the gaps when things weren't going right. Van was incredibly agile on his feet and nothing seemed to have fazed him. If Van had a bad moment on camera he never let it show and it was his humor often got him through some difficult moments and the audience likely never knew it.

What you saw of Van was what you got, I'm sure you have seen that by now Rob…there is nothing artificial about him. Van was always a happy presence in the newsroom…even when he first met me it was like he always knew me…like we were always friends and like I said he was never fazed by anything. He was so talented that he handled everything so smoothly and easily. Van made everything he did look easy that was one of the great gifts that Van has always had…if there was pressure he never showed it. Now as far as how folks remember him well he did many, many shows such as It's Academic and numerous bowling shows but he will always be remembered as the Voice of the Bills. He did the Stallions the Bisons and the Braves but he is the man…the voice who made the memories. He made those great moments come alive and there is nothing in my mind that exceeds that when thinking about what Van gave the radio audience. Van was the king of his field…it was sad when he left the microphone behind and we miss him a lot in the newsroom.

I did work Vans last broadcast and we had set aside two minutes for his good-bye …now I can't recall all that he said, he rode Don Paul of course but I do remember his last few words as being…his last 6 p.m. newscast his final on air words were…Vic you cut me off again…Lou fire that guy!

CHAPTER THIRTEEN

You feel on top of the world with all your nice friends. But mind it, it's very difficult
to have great friends who stand beside you for the rest of your life.
-Anonymous-

Van, many New Yorkers have grown up with you. They have listened to you call game after game and they watched you nightly for over forty years. You made for them, for us, for me so many memories and you were always there for us all. When you are called part of our families, what does that mean to you?

Rob I hope I have been respectful and I hope I have entertained and informed. That's certainly what I have always enjoyed and something that I always wanted to do is to entertain. I learned early on in life that at the end of the day...at the end of our lives that we should be sure to have at least six good friends that way we don't have to rent our pall-bearers.

True you want to be sure there's enough players on the field that day don't you?

Oh God yes. It's not hard to be friendly. In today's world everyone walks around with a scowl and seldom do neighbors know each other. I like to talk...I will stop and talk to anyone who wants to listen and even if they don't want to listen I'll start up a conversation. I have been made to feel like I am part of everyone's family; certainly being called Uncle Van has endeared me to many. I don't know where I got the nickname from...it does seem like I have always been called Uncle Van and that has suited me just fine. I like being considered a part of everyone's family or to be seen in such a good light that people will consider me their adopted uncle.

My Uncle Paul was my favorite, he taught me a lot of things. He made me laugh and smile and always seemed to smile when times were hard for him. I think that might be how people remember you; you always made them smile and forget things for a couple of hours.

You know Rob that uncles and grandfathers are considered wise and all-knowing and I certainly wasn't always right and I know I made many mistakes over the years but I wanted to leave you all with some short comments and observations. First about the game that I love, I did want to say that not only I, but the city of Buffalo and for that matter the National Football League owes so much to Ralph Wilson Jr. Ralph Wilson was the one who saw Buffalo as a major league city, he made it a major league city long before The Buffalo Sabers and The Buffalo Braves came to town and he is the only owner to bring a Championship to the city of Buffalo.

As we have discussed Rob, Ralph Wilson stepped forward early on in the history of the American Football League and literally saved two of the now most storied franchises from going under financially, the Oakland Raiders and the then Boston Patriots. Those teams may well not have ever been before the football fans now if not for what Ralph Wilson did for them in the '60s. Ralph Wilson could have taken his team…the Bills to larger markets, he had his opportunities to do this many times, he said no thank you and he kept the Bills in Buffalo. The fans of the Buffalo Bills owe this time of year to Ralph Wilson, he could have moved the team and number of times but he didn't. It's nice to be told that I gave so many memories to the fans but Ralph perhaps is responsible for them certainly more than me…he's the boss…he made the choices and he made them always with the fans in Buffalo in mind.

We all know the Bills have had some pretty bad seasons. They went through some very difficult years here, 1-13 seasons early and some two and three win seasons but Ralph Wilson with the help of Bill Polian they must be rightfully credited in putting together one of the all time great teams ever to take to the field. The Buffalo Bills of the Super Bowl years, in my opinion we will never, never see such a team ever again just take a look at these names: Jim Kelly Hall of Fame, James Lofton Hall of Fame, Thurman Thomas Hall of Fame, Bruce Smith Hall of Fame, Andre Reed a very likely Hall of Fame member. Remember that offensive line of Hull, Richter and "House" Ballard and Steve Tasker perhaps the best Special Teams player ever.

It was truly an amazing collection of players and Ralph wrote the checks, he kept them together and brought some of the most exciting football ever to be seen in the history of the

National Football League right here to our back yard…it's about time that he has been rightfully recognized for all his work. I am so proud to have called him "boss" and will always be proud to call him friend that is for damn sure.

Van with Ralph Wilson on Vans final day.

The fans…and this is hard…they have always been there in bad and in the good…they have always been supportive of the Bills and of me. They, you are my friends too; you will always be my friends. I haven't forgot that support for me. When I am told that I was part of their families well I consider them a part of mine too. They are my friends…no fan has ever been a stranger to me and even today Rob when I leave a game and someone asks to take my picture I'll say to them that it's me who wants my picture taken with them. I hoped they enjoyed my work.

I hope at the end of the day the fans…all of them appreciated my effort. I never missed a game and I think I was always there for the fans. I know though at times when the team was bad that some fans wanted to get rid of everybody associated with the Bills, Ralph, the head coach, the ball-boys and the guys in the booth…me. I enjoyed and enjoy every minute with them and I have wondered…since so many years have now gone passed if they haven't forgotten about me but when I am at the store or coming out of a game the fans are always there to say hey Van…we miss you Van…it does me good I tell you…and we miss you all too.

They have told me so many times that they remember listening to me when they were kids and then their children listened to me call Bills games or a Braves game and I can assure all of them... all of the fans that you were always there for me too...from the early days to my final game in the booth alongside John you have been my friends through it all and I can never say thank you enough for giving me and Gloria so many special moments.

Rob I do kid a lot but the women in my life have been the greatest of my allies...from my mother and grandmother to my wife Gloria. They are and have all been my iron women and Gloria my wife is a remarkable woman. We have been married now 57. Just one more quick story and this one is regarding Gloria's father...her father was an amazing man in his own right.

Her family came from Russia and her father had actually escaped from the Russian Naval Academy...as a boy he had even met Grigori Rasputin the "Mad Monk"...a psychic but some said he was a thorn in the side of the Tsars and had actually led to their downfall. The memory of meeting Rasputin stayed with him the remainder of his life. Anyway Gloria's father walked away from the Russian Navy when he was in Singapore. It was either at the outbreak or in the midst of The Russian Revolution...regardless he escaped during the Russian Revolution because everyone and anyone who had even a drop of royal blood was being eliminated and there is Russian royal blood in Gloria's family. He jumped ship and found his way...all the way to Long Island. When he got here he had an apple in one hand and a dime in his pocket. He had absolutely nothing. He was a brilliant, hard workingman and it wasn't long before he had found the right circle of friends and professional acquaintances and he soon went into business with Sikorsky.

Van is that Igor Sikorsky as in the helicopter inventor Sikorsky?

Yes the guy who invented the helicopter...well he was at least a pioneer in the helicopter and in fixed wing aircraft. He had had many hits and misses in its development but he got it right and he grew his company establishing Sikorsky Manufacturing Corporation there on Long Island. Gloria is from Long Island her father would come to work for the company. He grew with the company...he was smart and worked hard and during the outbreak of World War Two he was working for Johnson, Drake and Piper which was one of the worlds largest engineering firms. Johnson, Drake and Piper along with the Army Corps of Engineers would be responsible for developing the fortifications in North Africa used in warding off "The

Desert Fox" Rommel. Her father would eventually have 30,000 Egyptians working for him during the war.

Now one day as he was sitting in a café in Cairo and a man approached him and said to him…you look very familiar do we know one anther her fathers introduced himself with the last name Michael Chaiko…the man in the café said I know a Fedia Chaiko who is in the French underground. Michael said my brother's name is Fedia. Fedia Chaiko was Gloria's uncle and it was believed that he had been killed during the Russian Revolution because of the royal bloodline.

The two were eventually reunited and Fedia moved to the states and became an artist…he was a quite a painter. Gloria's father was later able to trace his brother's footsteps back to 1916 after they lost track of each other during the Russian Revolution. It was quite a story and after the Second World War to the states and he became an illustrator for Hallmark and for children's books and designed incredible pieces of work. He married a girl Alexandria and they opened a shop in Manhattan and lived happily ever after. As a matter of fact he had to go to Gloria's father to ask permission to get married but it was quite a story of a family reunion.

Rob there is another story about her father. After the war he became a builder down on Long Island and for several years he won the award for builder of the year. He was a builder of high-end homes and one of the homes he built was for a guy named Douvan. Gloria's family had this yacht and we would always go down there and spend days on it…it was a fantastic time.

They always had parties and this one time there was a party being thrown and we attended, Gloria and I were dating at the time and when we got there the yard and home was filled with as many people that could be fit in and the Douvan family was there…it may have been at their home. I remember this one evening clearly for several reasons but one was because there was this little blonde girl who was there she was 7 or 8 years old…her mother was Mary Douvan. She, this little girl was running around and jumping here and there and hanging on to me and inviting me to play games of all kinds. She was a cute little blonde girl and we learned that she was already doing some modeling for magazines and stores and each every time we went there she would be looking for her Uncle Van. We'd play and she just seemed to take to me like I was a long lost member of the family.

Gloria near the boats of Long Island circa 1954.

Anyway she would hang onto me and was just so outgoing, most kids are always shy around strangers but she wasn't that way and this one night when we were there her mother said Sandy it's time to go to bed…say good night to everyone and get up to bed. I think her name was Alexandra but they called her Sandy for short. Well she said goodnight planted a big ol' kiss on my cheek and went up to bed while the rest of the Russian's stayed up all night drinking Vodka, Champaign and just about anything they could lay their hands on. I left at the crack of dawn and they were still going at it.

Anyway little Sandy went up to bed and that was all I thought about it until just about ten years later probably longer when Gloria's sister calls and tells her this…she said Gloria you'll never believe what happened…what happened Gloria asked…well…her sister asks if she remembers the Douvan family and the dinners we use to have there down on Long Island…yes of course Gloria answered. Do you remember that little girl Sandy? Of course Gloria said…well her sister goes on to say that little Sandy had gone on to make a couple of movies…Gidget and Summer Place but that she has changed her name from Alexandra to Sandra…Sandra Dee. So I have always been able to claim that I was kissed by Sandra Dee before Bobby Darin ever was. That is the story, a couple of stories about Gloria's father he was simply amazing and so of course is my bride.

Gloria has been by my side for it all, we met while at Fredonia State and through it all, the tough days, all the games all the fun she has been by my side and been my best buddy. We have been blessed to have traveled the world and see and meet many, many wonderful people.

We have had a lot if fun and shared many adventures. I can't say the job I did was really work because I loved what I did. I worked hard early on so as to give something back to my mother. I was blessed to have always had strong, amazingly strong women in my life, my mother and grandmother and my wife Gloria. Sometimes I don't know what else to say other than I have been blessed. To my children Cathryn, Van Jr. and to you Gloria thanks for the smiles, laughs and unending dedication and love.

Van and Gloria

Cathryn, Van and Van Michael

CONCLUSION

Jack Ramsay was the best of any of the coaches that I ever had the pleasure of broadcasting their games. He is a tremendous coach, broadcaster and friend.

Dr. Jack, as many affectionately refer to him, holds a Doctorate in Education from the University of Pennsylvania. He may be best known for leading the Portland Trailblazers to their 1976-1977 championship and for his broadcast work with the Indiana Pacers, Miami Heat and ESPN, but he is also a member of the Pro Basketball Hall of Fame and is in the top ten winning coaches of all time. In 1955 he became head coach of the Saint Joseph Hawks, from which he was alum. In 1968 he was hired as the head coach of the Philadelphia 76ers and would later coach the Indiana Pacers, Portland Trailblazers and from 1972-1976 he was the head coach of the Buffalo Braves.

Rob I do still travel quite a bit, especially this time of year. I cover numerous NBA training. I was just in Indiana and then down in Memphis for several days covering the Memphis Grizzlies and after Memphis I went down to Houston for treatment on my cancer…it's a condition some may know about and some may not. I'm doing well, it's been three years since they have found anything…it's a wonderful hospital that I go to called MD Anderson…former Bills quarterback Joe Ferguson may go there as well for what he was undergoing.

I have to say that I am so pleased that Van's story—a comprehensive story is being written. As comprehensive as a story on Van can be because there is so much—obviously he is one of the greatest, if not the greatest, NFL play-by-play men of all times. He had a knack of injecting his own personal enthusiasm about the team and the game into the broadcast that was unique at the time. It is unique now. He knew the game of basketball well, because I think that he was a very competitive athlete himself. He was a great tennis player too as Van and I played tennis all the time and Van certainly loved basketball, and loving a sport obviously

*helped him in broadcasting the games at the college level and when he broadcasted our games
with the Buffalo Braves. He was a terrific competitor himself, which helped him succeed.
Van—if I remember when we played tennis, he played left-handed and he had some injury to
his left arm and learned to play right-handed or vice versa, and he was a fantastic tennis player
with the other hand. He was very competitive, though I couldn't convince him to take a bike
ride with me, probably because I ride a hundred miles at a time.*

Van did mention that you were a tri-athlete and once rode your bike from
Indiana to Ocean City, New Jersey.

*Yes I did. I was coaching the Indiana Pacers at the time, the mid-eighties. I'm 84 years
old now so I was 63 or 64 years old then. Ocean City is just south of Atlantic City. I was
doing triathlons and the bike rides were a significant part of the triathlon and at the start of
the season I'd talk back and forth with the players and five or so of them said 'yeah, Doc,
we'll take the ride with you.' The season moved along and before I knew it there was only one
guy going to make the ride and that was me. And so I rode my bike some 700 miles. One by
one they, the much younger athletes all dropped out as the day for the bike ride approached.*

Coach if we could get a little additional background, please. You attended
St. Joseph's College?

*I went there—it's St. Joseph's University now— and I went there in the fall of 1942
and after a year I went into the service. I went into the Navy and the Navy sent me into their
officer-training program, which required a two-year period in college, so they sent me to
Villanova for a year and then to Columbia University in New York City. After which I was
then sent into the more active side of World War Two.*

You served the tail end of the war as an Ensign?

*Yes I was, and I served in the Pacific. I joined the underwater demolition teams, which were
the forerunner of the Navy Seals. I did most of my service with them and I was part of a group
that was to rendezvous and prepare for the invasion of Japan. There were thirty teams with a
hundred men in each group and we were all prepared for the invasion of Japan when the Atomic
Bomb was dropped and they then sent us home. It was over with two bombs. After the war I*

went back to St. Joseph's and finished my degree there and started high school coaching. During that time I completed my Doctorate at the University of Pennsylvania and received a chance to be a coach at St. Joseph's. I took that and coached there for eleven years. Then I went into the NBA first as the general manager for the 76ers and after two years became the team's coach and stayed there for four years. Then I coached the Buffalo Braves for four years and then to Portland for ten years and finished off my coaching with a couple of years at Indiana.

I remember your time with the Braves, of course, but remember the championship team with the Trailblazers just as much because of Bill Walton.

Sure Bill was the MVP of the series and we did beat a good Philadelphia, they had Julius Erving, Henry Bibby and Doug Collins among the many.

If you hadn't gotten into coaching, what would you have done?

Honestly I don't know. At first my concentration was pre-med. I thought I wanted to be a doctor and of course we had all the undergraduate courses in biology and chemistry and we had all the labs that went with them. But for me to complete the labs I'd have to miss some practices. Now, it was okay with my coaches but it wasn't okay with me and I said to myself that if I wanted to play basketball more than I wanted to study to be a doctor, then I hadn't made the right career choice.

You have written a couple of books; one was, *Dr. Jack's Leadership Lessons Learned From a Lifetime in Basketball.* What would you say the top couple of lessons are?

I believe that a well-balanced teamwork, preparation and performance approach is and will be successful in not only sports, but in everything someone chooses to do in life. In my case it was basketball. A person has to prepare him or herself because there is going to be a lot of competition in whatever you do and proper preparation will help you get the job done well under any amount of duress.

When did you and Van first meet?

Van and Dr. Jack, courtesy of Steve Cichon.

I met Van the day I took the job in Buffalo and I immediately saw someone who loved his job. He was very much a consummate professional when it came to broadcasting. I came to Buffalo in the third year of the team's history and they hadn't won anything. They were winning 20, 21 or 22 games a year, which meant they were losing 60. I knew a lot of changes had to be made, and we made them, and in the second year we went from 21 to 42 wins. We knew Bob McAdoo could play, but he, too, was part of that 21-win season and we knew that Randy Smith could play and we felt that Bob Kauffman could contribute, but that was it and we got rid of everyone else or nearly everyone else and added nine new players.

Van, even in those bad days, was enthusiastic about the team and an incredible pleasure to be around. And Van and I had a lot of fun. You may have heard this one story: Van loved airports. He would get that twinkle in his eyes anytime we walked through an airport, and he would deliberately look for the passengers returning from Hawaii. He was devilish to say it simply. He would go up to these passengers returning from Hawaii and he'd say, 'Folks, hi, we are having a pineapple inspection so everyone who is bringing a pineapple home with them needs to line up against the wall here and we will need to inspect your pineapples.' All these passengers would line up against a wall and Van would tell them a couple of things and conclude by saying that he would be right back. Of course, Van would disappear and never return leaving these folks standing in line to have their pineapples inspected. He did this every flight, but his favorite was the earring line. Wherever we were, he'd go up to a woman and so deliberately ask where had her other earring gone and of course, without pause they'd all always reach for it.

The seventies was a meager, slim pickings period of time. The Sabres were new and the Bills weren't at their best. The Braves were both exciting and new. Do you think the NBA could make it again in Buffalo?

Well, I don't think so. A city needs to be able to fill an arena every night with eighteen to twenty thousand people. They need major sponsors and they have to be able to compete money-wise for good players. It's tough. Buffalo has already been on the defensive about everything; they are the brunt of so many jokes, so when their sports teams do well, it's a way of sayings 'see, I told you so.'

Buffalo though, I have always loved the people and the city. I was welcomed there warmly and made many friends and Van was, and is on the top of that list. I would think that broadcasters who have listened to Van Miller would always be able to learn from him. I would hope too that students in communications would be able to study Van and on how to be a broadcaster. There was and is none better than Van. I think he is a model for broadcasters of any sport. He has a great voice; he has the ultimate rhythm; he knew the sport so well and he was as well aware of any sport and every game as any of the players and coaches ever were. Buffalo is fortunate to call him theirs. Broadcasting is blessed to have had him be a part their fraternity. He is a tremendous man and I was fortunate to have met him when I did, and I will always be fortunate and blessed to call him my dear friend.

"We miss you all too."

Breinigsville, PA USA
27 November 2009
228249BV00001BA/31/P